101 IDEAS FOR UPSTAIRS

Published by BBC Books
BBC Worldwide Ltd, Woodlands,
80 Wood Lane, London W12 0TT

First published for
Marks & Spencer in 2003
This edition published in 2005
Copyright © BBC Worldwide 2003

ISBN 0 563 52258 5

Edited by Joanna Simmons

Commissioning Editor: Vivien Bowler
Project Editor: Julia Zimmermann
Series Design: Claire Wood
Book Design: Kathryn Gammon
Design Managers: Sarah Ponder and
Annette Peppis
Production Controller: Christopher Tinker

Set in Amasis MT and ITC Officina Sans
Printed and bound in Italy by LEGO SpA
Colour origination by Butler & Tanner

BBC Worldwide would like to thank the
following for providing photographs and
permission to reproduce copyright material.
While every effort has been made to trace
and acknowledge all copyright holders, we
would like to apologize should there have
been any errors or omissions.

All photographs © *BBC Good Homes*
magazine 2003 with the exception of:
Armitage Shanks 149, 155, 157, 159,
203, 209; Ideal Standard 181, 197;
Twyford Bathrooms 153

BBC
BOOKS

101 IDEAS FOR UPSTAIRS
BEDROOM, BATHROOM

Julie Savill

BBC
GoodHomes

CONTENTS

BEDROOMS

BATHROOMS

INTRODUCTION

When it comes to decorating, what's needed is bags of inspiration, a spare weekend or two, and plenty of planning. It's the time you spend thinking and dreaming about what you want that will really pay off in the long run. Put in the effort now and you can be sure that the room you end up with will suit your needs and your taste and be a real pleasure to use.

If you are currently viewing your bedroom or bathroom with a look of less than total satisfaction on your face then this book is for you. In it we've gathered together 101 of the most stylish, desirable and achievable decorating schemes guaranteed to kick-start your plans for your upstairs rooms. Ideas for bedrooms and bathrooms are neatly divided into style sections but I would recommend browsing through from cover to cover because

you never know where your next good idea is going to come from and all the schemes are there to be copied wholesale or mixed and matched to make a look that is entirely individual and personal.

Once you've settled on a style, whether it's cutting edge contemporary or elegantly traditional the next task is to make a list of all the functions a room has to fulfil. A bedroom is first and foremost somewhere to sleep, but it's also a dressing room so you'll need storage and mirrors, a TV and reading room so lighting is crucial and should ideally be flexible, and it's possibly the place you tuck yourself away when you want a little 'me-time'. With all this information to hand you can start planning your new scheme on paper, fitting in all the elements and making lists of what you have and are going to keep and what you want and will need to source and buy.

The most exciting part is when you get down to planning the actual colour scheme, choosing shades for walls, fabrics for curtains and soft furnishings. The best way to ensure success is to make yourself a colour board. It's the way our team of stylists plan colour schemes for *BBC Good Homes* magazine and it takes all the guesswork out of the process. You'll need a large piece of white card or paper and some glue then away you go. Gather together samples of all the materials, paints and floor coverings you are considering using then arrange them on the card. It's quite easy to see in this way which shades and patterns look pleasing together and which ones jar. Keep trying different combinations until you find a mix that looks right to you, because at the end of the day this is your room and you are the only one who is to say that a scheme works or not!

Julie Savill, Editor
BBC Good Homes magazine

The look: Blues in every shade, from bold to soft lilac, give this bedroom a refreshing, dip-in-the-sea feel. Blue is calming and relaxed, the perfect shade to help clear your mind at the end of the day.

Walls: Painting one wall a vibrant shade is a great way to breathe life into a plain room. Then team it with walls in soft lilac and white to keep the scheme feeling light and relaxed. When picking a bold blue, choose one with purple tones that will add warmth – pure blues, like strong navy, can look very stark.

Bed: With its dark-coloured wall, layering up the bed with pretty blue shades is key to the success of this room. It helps lift the whole mood and gives it a delicate, feminine feel. Here, classic white bedlinen has been piled up with throws and quilts in lilac, misty blue, softest green and silvery shades. You can mix in as many colours as you like, as long as they're all the same strength, otherwise the subtle layered effect will be spoilt by a dominant shade.

Window: To keep the room feeling light and peaceful, a light-filtering, sheer blind is hung at the window. A pretty spot-and-line pattern shares all the same colours as the bedding, for a coordinated, easy-on-the-eye look.

Furniture: A chair makes a good bedside table, if you have space, with the added bonus that you can hang bags, towels or throws from its back. This junkshop chair has been made over to match the painted floorboards and fire surround, looking crisp and smart.

The look: This simple, modern room relies on three key ingredients: calming white on walls, floor and at the window, sleek, contemporary furniture in metal and glass, and a brightly coloured quilt in shimmering silk. An all-white scheme can look very austere and clinical, especially when teamed with modern furniture, but just by throwing a colourful quilt over the bed, you can warm up the look and create a vibrant focus.

Floor: Soften the blow of getting up in the morning with a soft, toe-tickling carpet. Keep the colour pale and neutral, but to add subtle interest, choose one from the huge range of woven textured carpets on the market today. This one has a thick bubbleweave that not only feels great, but looks beautiful, too.

Furniture: Pared-down and pale, the furniture in this room is unashamedly modern. A metal and glass console doubles both as dressing table and television stand while a sleek wardrobe fitted with frosted glass tones in beautifully. If you like this look, choose pieces in metal, glass, plastic or Perspex, and avoid wooden furniture, which instantly darkens a room scheme.

Curtains: To ensure a peaceful night's sleep, line curtains with blackout material. For a lavish look at tall windows, be generous with fabric, allowing extra length so you can generously drape it in a 'puddle' on the floor.

Storage: Every bedroom needs storage, but in a clean, light room like this, a bulky chest of drawers or vast wardrobe would look out of place. Instead, choose pieces that work hard. This sleek wardrobe offers both hanging and drawer space, while room under the bed that would otherwise be redundant is filled with a row of storage boxes, ideal for stashing shoes, bedlinen and out-of-season clothes.

The look: This colourful bedroom shouts contemporary cool. A graphic pattern painted onto walls in up-to-the-minute shades of lilac, purple and blue gives the room eye-catching style, and the same palette of shades is found on the bedlinen, giving the room a warm, gently coordinated feel.

The wall: To create a multi-coloured wall like this one, start by painting the entire wall one colour – ideally the lightest shade. When it's dry, mask off areas to be painted in other shades. Mask off a variety of shapes – lines, rectangles, squares – to give the wall energy, then apply two coats of emulsion paint to each block and leave to dry. Peel off the tape and repeat to create more blocks of colour, overlapping them in some places.

Bedlinen: To keep the colourful theme, a stripy pink duvet cover and pillowcases jazz up the bed. A couple of bright cushions add further pizzazz, while a lilac throw ties in perfectly with the main colour on the wall and helps calm the colours down.

Storage: A tall shelf unit, tucked into an alcove, provides plenty of storage. It's ideal for a teenager's bedroom because it has space for files, school books and a stereo – objects you might not find in a less hardworking adult bedroom.

Artwork: Inexpensive, widely available, and made in hundreds of eye-catching designs, contemporary wrapping paper makes a pretty poster above the bed. Frame it in a simple glass clip-frame for a more professional look.

The look: This room is a modern-day take on Native American style. The bed has a metal headboard with a stepped Navaho design and is layered with deeply-coloured fringed throws and tasselled rugs for a cosy, North American look.

Colour: Colours are drawn from a simple, natural palette: palest blue on the walls (a good, neutral backdrop), sand, sky-blue and green-grass shades on the bed. It gives the room freshness and a feeling of calm. You could be camping out on the wide plains, watching a herd of buffalo file past (well, almost).

Bed: This Native American-style bed sets the scene for the whole room and needs little more than a few textiles to complete the look. The hand-forged wrought-iron panel uses a stepped Navaho motif and looks striking against the simple pale blue walls. For textured cosiness, blankets and small-fringed rugs are piled up on the bed with cushions and pillows in blue and sand scattered over.

Accessories: These are key to creating a unified and success-ful look. Less is more, though, remember, and here metal coat hooks that echo the shape of the bedstead and some black and white photos of fitting scenes continue the Native American idea without making the room feel too themed.

Window: Simple cream curtains, clipped to a wire curtain rail, get a dash of interest by glueing or sew-ing feathers to them along the top. Most haberdashery shops sell feathers, but make sure you choose long, natural-coloured ones (rather than dyed) for the best effect.

CONTEMPORARY

The look: Forget minimalism. These days it's hip to love glamour. Shimmering fabrics, sensual materials, sequins and beadwork are all the rage in home wares, and it's a look that this bedroom has mastered beautifully. To keep it classy, the basics of the scheme are smart and plain, while the bed is a mass of silky quilts and decadent cushions.

Colours: The base colours here are soft and organic. Taupe and cream on the walls, a padded, mushroom-coloured bed and a soft brown rug create a warm background. Then, to up the luxe factor, more exotic shades are layered on top – brilliant, kingfisher blue, rich mossy green and glistening oyster.

Walls: Make a statement with a dramatic striped wall. Bands of colour in similar tones are easy to paint on. First paint your wall with a couple of coats of your paler colour. When it's dry, use a plumb line and pencil to draw vertical lines, then stick low-tack masking tapes along the lines and carefully paint on your second colour with a roller. For added opulence, use gloss stripes over a matt paint.

Furniture: All the pieces in this room shout contemporary style. The bedstead is upholstered in mink-soft fabric, and next to it stands a sleek, simple console table, perfect for drinks, books and other bedtime essentials.

Bedlinen: Layering colours and textures creates an instantly luxurious look. Here, a mohair throw rubs shoulders with a couple of satin quilts and a smattering of beautiful beaded and sequined cushions.

The look: A combination of pale grey walls, white bedlinen and clean lines gives this bedroom a contemporary but comfortable feel. Minimal furniture and some striking artwork mean the room has a strong identity but manages to avoid a fussy feel.

Colour: This room is anchored by three key colours: pale grey, chocolate-brown and white. By sticking to a limited colour scheme like this, you can be sure your room will look strong and coordinated, not hectic. Here, units and photo frames in the same grey as the walls look discreet and simple, dark wooden floorboards add warmth and white bedlinen looks contemporary and clean, softening the lines of the starkly modern bed.

Bedlinen: The all-white bedding gets a lift with the addition of a waffle throw. If you love white but worry that it can look boring, try mixing in different textures, as here, to add some interest and variety. This throw is draped casually over the end of the bed, but you can still see under it, which helps give the room a spacious feel.

Artwork: These Russian Revolution propaganda prints, neatly framed in black, look graphic and striking on this wall. If you have a narrow wall, try running a line of prints right across it, as here. The horizontal line can help make the wall seem wider than it is.

Lighting: An adjustable lamp, so typically used on a desk, is perfect by a bed, too. Direct it over the bed for night-time reading, or direct the head away or upwards to create softer, ambient light.

The look: This spacious bedroom gets plenty of light and so it suits a fresh, contemporary colour scheme. An iron bed frame provides a nod to 19th-century style, but otherwise, the room is all about fuss-free modern living.

Colour: To make the most of the light that floods this room, the walls are painted a pale blue shade but are given depth and energy by a border of deep navy above the high picture rail. This is a great, no-risk way of adding richer colour to your room, as it won't dominate the space, but will give it more character.

Furniture: Furniture is kept to a minimum, to accentuate the room's generous dimensions and continue the light, fresh feel. The cast-iron bed creates a stunning centrepiece and its classic style is given a modern boost with bedlinen and a throw in bright shades of turquoise and green. A small, modern unit on castors functions as a multi-functional bedside table and can be wheeled to another location to free-up space.

Floor: Original floorboards, sanded smooth and varnished, are hard-wearing and handsome, but in a bedroom, where you tend to walk barefoot, it's a good idea to add a rug or two to soften them and provide some warm texture underfoot. This sheepskin rug tones in with the white in the duvet cover and is super-soft and sensual.

Accessories: Just like the furniture, accessories have been kept to a minimum here to help the room feel unfussy and modern. Just one simple print on the wall is enough, as the colour provides plenty of interest on its own. A few family photos help personalize the space and potted daffodils or houseplants make a natural, lush addition.

The look: This bedroom is blessed with lots of natural light, and a simple pure white scheme makes the most of it. Fitted shelves give an alcove a new purpose and a simple roller blind and white duvet cover add to the unfussy, cool feel.

Colour: White is a safe bet for any room. It maximizes light, looks fresh and clean and can be teamed with any colour. In a room that gets lots of light, pure brilliant white looks great and is an inexpensive, easy-to-get-hold-of solution. In darker rooms, try a subtly off-white shade to add a little warmth. Pure brilliant white has optical brighteners added to it and is slightly shot through with blue, which can make it look cold.

Shelves: If you have a room with recesses or an alcove, fitting shelves into them is one of the most useful things you can do, creating storage and filling a space that might otherwise be useless. Here, chunky white shelves are stacked with books, vases and pictures to add colour and personality to the room.

Window: Roller blinds are a simple, unfussy window treatment and suit this clean scheme perfectly. Here, blackout fabric has been used to help keep out unwelcome early morning rays.

Furniture: If you like to watch television in bed, try storing it on a neat trolley like this one, so you can move it around to get the best view. And don't be afraid to mix old and new. Although most of the furniture here is modern and pale, an antique French chair sits by the archway, its sensual shape emphasized by the clean lines of its surroundings.

The look: This is modern glamour at its best. Sumptuous textiles and glassy, polished surfaces create a chic and sophisticated look. This room is about comfort with a hint of luxury. Clutter is kept to a minimum, colours are bleached out and beautiful, and there's a light, airy feel.

Furniture: A console and side table gain extra glamour points by being treated to two coats of high-gloss paint. This creates a shiny, lacquered effect that's smart and modern. Add mirror panels to drawers as a finishing touch – ask a glazier to cut some to size and stick them in place with glass adhesive. Glass knobs complete the look.

Colour: To create a cool modern look in the bedroom, blend soft shades of clear turquoise, dusky mauve and soothing taupe. Add a splash of colour with cushions or pillowcases in rich grape. These small doses of colour will be easier to live with than if you paint a whole wall a bold shade, and you can change the cushions from time to time to refresh the look. Keep walls pale and add a soft carpet in a taupe shade that will be gentle on your feet and won't show dirt easily.

Bedlinen: For an opulent feel, layer the bed with sheets, throws and bedspreads. The satin eiderdown is a classic piece that has made a big fashion comeback lately and adds a touch of luxury to this otherwise simple scheme. Scatter over a few silk and sequined cushions to add a little shimmer and sparkle.

Curtains: To keep the light, cool feel, choose a curtain fabric that's fine and filmy. Stick to a discreet design, like this subtle repeat pattern of flower heads – just enough detail to add interest at the windows, without dominating the room and drawing the eye away from the glossy furniture and luxurious bed.

The look: This contemporary room has a stylish, low-level bed as its centrepiece. Warm toffee colours, a mix of textures and plenty of honey-coloured wood are key ingredients to this relaxed modern look.

Colour: This neutral palette mixes soft cream, oatmeal and mushroom colours with the golden brown of beech wood. A textured coir carpet provides the base note to the scheme, while the creamy curtains add a sunny feel at the window.

Texture: Mixing in lots of different textures is a great way to add depth and interest to a neutral scheme, which can look a little dull otherwise. Here, a woven coir carpet is rough and fibrous, while a shiny ivory satin eiderdown adds a shot of shine and glamour. No opportunity is missed to add some texture – even the cushions have knobs on – and instead of a traditional flat-weave fabric, the curtains are made from woollen cable-knit throws, the kind you'd more usually find draped over a double bed or sofa.

Furniture: Low beds are big style news at the moment and this one has integrated side tables and a wide border around the frame that you can use as a handy shelf. A bed like this does need a good-sized room, however, to allow space for the platform design. In this room, it's teamed with a coffee table in similar coloured wood to keep the look coordinated.

Pictures: Pictures are displayed in stylish lines along a shelf that has a small lip to stop them slipping off. Simple beech frames complement the bare-wood look perfectly.

The look: Heavenly, soothing shades of lilac ease the mind and calm the senses – perfect for a tranquil bedroom. The mix of modern and contemporary bedding together with an old, decorative table and pretty lamp add to the laid-back, effortlessly stylish feel.

Colour: Lilac is famous for being a soothing, relaxing shade that creates a mood of spirituality and peace. If used on every wall, it can look a little heavy and its soothing quality is lost, so paint it on just one or two walls, or in an alcove, then use fresh white or palest purple elsewhere.

Bed: This upholstered bedstead is bang up-to-date, without looking edgy. Its soft material and smooth lines put comfort first, while the pale mink colour adds the only other shade to the room besides lilac – great for lightening the look and stopping it looking overly coordinated.

Bedlinen: To create a relaxing atmosphere, keep cushions and throws to a minimum, so the eye is not confused by a mass of things to look at, but glides over the whole scene. Here, white bedlinen with a pretty lilac and purple trim is teamed with a lilac suede cushion.

Furniture: The white table sits neatly in an alcove and breaks up the lilac wall nicely. A collection of feminine pieces – a glass lamp, vase, some pretty postcards – give this corner lots of personality without dominating the whole room. A squishy armchair covered in lilac fabric by the window is the perfect place to sit with a book. Who says bedrooms should be just for sleeping in?

The look: This airy attic conversion has plenty of unusual features. Ceilings are sloping and the brickwork of the chimneys of the house gives the room stacks of character. To these raw ingredients are added simple, contemporary furniture and a few decorative touches.

Colour: Although it's an attic room, this bedroom gets lots of natural light, thanks to a large window in the sloping roof. A pale shade of blue-grey has been painted onto the walls to make the most of this, creating a cool, fresh feel, and floorboards are painted white to help bounce light around.

Bedlinen: The bed is the centrepiece of this room, beautifully framed by sloping brickwork. To give it a luxurious feel, it's layered with cool white cotton, a shiny grey satin quilt and a smattering of silky cushions. The quilt picks up the grey of the walls, tying the room together, and its shimmery fabric adds to the light airy feel.

Furniture: In a room with sloping ceilings, it's very difficult to fit tall pieces like wardrobes or chests of drawers in. Here, a low sideboard – a piece typically found in a living or dining room – offers some storage and there's a neat armchair for relaxing. Clothes and bulky items are stored in another room. The bed occupies the tallest centre section of the room, so there's space to sit up in it.

Accessories: Weaving a few decorative accessories into a bedroom can lift the look from comfortable, to really individual. Here, a wirework chandelier adds a shot of elegance and glamour, while an abstract painting above the bed creates a focus for the eye, and uses colours that tie in with the room's soft grey and white colour scheme.

The look: A grown-up, glamour puss look is what this bedroom is all about. Simple, stylish furniture in white and cream, some stunning artwork, a splash of soft pink and sexy red and, hey presto, you've made yourself a bedroom that's drop-dead gorgeous.

Bed: A classic wrought-iron bedstead looks bang up-to-date painted soft cream. A simple combination of white sheets and cream blanket cover it, but it's given a shot of colour and style with a bright red bolster, tied at each end with lengths of plum satin ribbon. This look is smarter and more original than scatter cushions – and a lot neater, too. To make your own, just wrap fabric around an old single duvet or some wadding, or buy a bolster from a good department store.

Walls: The walls here are painted in two shades of pink. Painting just one wall in a rich colour is a great way of introducing a strong shade to your room without the risk of the colour dominating. Painting the remaining walls a soft, whitey-pink keeps the room feeling light. Create a focus on one wall by making your own stunning artwork. This picture has been made by getting a fashion image enlarged and printed onto canvas at a photography shop. Its colours suit the room perfectly.

Accessories: Colourful bags and scarves needn't all be hidden away. Here, draped on a modern coat stand, they make a pretty feature in one corner of the room. To keep clutter to a minimum so that chosen accessories stand out, a tall chest of drawers and a deep chest, all in pale painted wood, provide lots of storage. Instead of draping fairy lights around the bedstead, they're given a home inside a glass vase – a neat way to display them.

The look: This bedroom combines warm woollens, duck-egg blue and plump pillows to create a tranquil nesting ground. The large feather scroll makes a striking focal point while simple stitching on the bedding continues the theme.

Colour: Duck-egg blue is subtle, warm and very versatile. It brings tranquility to any room, and teams perfectly with white for a soothing, contemporary scheme. Here, a pale carpet, white table and headboard add freshness, while bedding in tones of silver, grey and blue tie in with the colour on the wall.

Bed: A simple, modern frame with a fresh white headboard makes the perfect no-fuss backdrop for some comforting, sensual bedding. Cosy sheepskin, soft mohair and sexy silk combine beautifully, in colours to please the eye and textures to delight the skin.

Furniture: A simple, white wooden table stands beside the bed – just right for a cool, contemporary scheme like this. It's versatile, too. Fold it up and store it away if you want a change. The rush chest provides useful storage as do the maize baskets under the bed, making use of space that would otherwise be wasted.

Walls: The feather scroll looks dramatic and stylish on the wall, its blue matching the paint perfectly, so that it stands out without looking garish and doesn't jar with the peaceful atmosphere. If you're going to use a long artwork like this, leave the rest of the wall blank. Small pictures hung near it would look out of proportion.

CONTEMPORARY

The look: There's a rich, opulent feel to this room, created by mixing deep wine and grape colours with subtle off-whites. Pale walls and simple accessories keep the room looking chic and modern, while lacquered surfaces hint at Eastern elegance.

Colour: Colour is used cleverly here to create richness, without being overpowering. The reds and purples of the bedding are teamed with a headboard and side table in exotic lacquered red, but the off-white walls, pale curtains and a few bits of pale bedlinen added to the mix bring welcome lightness, so the room's overall feel is pleasantly airy and fresh.

Headboard: This bed has an unusual built-in headboard. A tall, boxy structure was made from MDF then painted a glossy red. It gives the bed a real no-nonsense presence in the room, and its top provides space for displaying favourite pieces, helping soften the look.

Side table: If you want to give your bedroom an exotic, Eastern feel, think lacquer. Here, an inexpensive, untreated wooden side table was given a few coats of lacquer paint for an intensely glossy, reflective look. To be authentic, choose black or blood red – classic Eastern shades.

Accessories: Symmetry is key to this bedroom's smart, contemporary look. On either side of the bed there is a lamp and candlestick, two matching artworks hang on the wall and a set of vases stand on top of the headboard. Displaying objects in this way creates a sense of order and balance, which can be softened by scattering cushions randomly over the bed.

CONTEMPORARY

The look: This room takes traditional bedroom ingredients like wallpaper and a wooden bed frame, and gives them a fresh, modern twist. Stripes are the theme, making a bold statement and helping this small room feel warm and full of character.

Colour: There's a lush, natural feel to the colours used here. Wallpaper with stripes in soft blue and cream create an interesting but muted backdrop, while a vibrant throw, quilt and cushion pick up the stripes theme and inject bright colour into the room with their strong greens, greys and turquoises. The floor is painted a neutral white to add freshness without detracting from the beautiful bedding.

Walls: Wallpaper went out of fashion a decade ago, but now it's back in style and better than ever. A soft stripe design adds subtle interest to the walls and helps a small room like this feel taller by elongating its walls.

Furniture: This wooden bed has a smart contemporary feel. The headboard's strong design and clean lines are set off by the mix of dark and pale wood. A simple square wooden shelf is fixed to the wall to serve as a bedside cabinet, leaving floor space free and so helping the room feel bigger.

Floor: Painting wooden floorboards white is an easy way to smarten them up and, unless they're very rough, there's no need to spend time sanding them first. By bouncing light around and creating a neutral backdrop, the floorboards give this small room a sense of airiness.

The look: This smart, sexy bedroom takes its inspiration from the velvety textures and rich, deep colours of autumn fruit. Sparkly glassware and layer upon layer of grape, berry and plum washed down with lashings of cream make for a perfect room recipe.

Colour: Taking centre stage are two lavish satin quilts in plum-red, purple and lilac, and a dyed sheepskin rug in matching plum. To help these dramatic shades sing out, the walls and carpet have been kept a pale ivory. Lilac curtains, pillowcases and artwork add subtle colour, softening the impact of the dramatic throws.

Furniture: The quilts are the most eye-catching ingredient, so the furniture has been kept solid and simple, with matching pieces used to stop the room becoming over-complicated. A tall chest of drawers in warm wood provides ample storage and a matching bedside table tones in. The wrought-iron bed frame looks elegant, and for a neat, coordinated look, there's a wrought-iron curtain pole, too.

Window: Simple, tab-top curtains are made from silk, then layered with sheer voiles to look just like the bloom on a juicy plum. The colour ties in beautifully with the shiny purples on the two-tone quilt.

Floor: A white carpet creates a snowy backdrop for the colourful quilts and rug. It has a knobbly, woven texture, which adds interest and depth to the pale colour. A dyed sheepskin rug breaks up the white and adds further luxury to this super-comfortable bedroom.

The look: Four-poster beds rank first for decadence and fun and they can take almost any kind of makeover or styling. This bed has been given a colonial look with lengths of split bamboo, bedlinen in crisp white and bold navy and a dash of brilliant red.

Bed: This sturdy, teak-toned four-poster has been given a simple makeover with lengths of bamboo screen from a garden centre. It has been fixed in place with wire, securely twisted through the bamboo and around the pole. Long pieces of red ribbon are attached to the top poles and used to secure the rolled-up bamboo.

Accessories: For this look, think sultry nights, exotic verandas dotted with glossy leaved palms and a fan whirring overhead. A palm has been used here to capture that feel, standing in a bright blue ceramic pot that tones in with the bedding. A woven chest completes the look, suggesting far-flung travels and supplying lots of useful storage.

Colour: The natural colour of bamboo is teamed with smart navy textiles and cushions and mixed with a dash of crisp white. To give the look heaps of energy and drama, splashes of red are added with the ribbons and a bright, circular rug. This red blends beautifully with the warm tones of the teak bed frame.

Flooring: Wooden floors are big style news these days and have lots of practical advantages, too. They're easy to clean, hygienic (great if you suffer from dust allergies) and hard-wearing. In a bedroom, though, it's a good idea to soften boards with a rug. You're likely to be walking around barefoot in here, so soft textures underfoot are welcome.

The look: This bedroom has used zingy orange to give it an up-to-the-minute feel. A few clever tricks like re-covering a plain headboard and painting the floorboards give the room bags of individuality, too.

Colour: Not a conventional colour in the bedroom, orange is bright, modern and invigorating. Team it with plenty of cream or white to cool it down. Here, plain white bedding, cream walls and cherry wood furniture help balance it, and give the look some grown up sophistication.

The headboard: A plain headboard has been covered with a soft, open-weave blanket to give it plenty of get up and glow. Cut a piece large enough to fold in half and fit over the entire headboard. Fold, then stitch the sides together. Turn right-side-out, press, then slide over the headboard.

Floor: Stripped floorboards have been given a wake-up call with a splash of fresh white and a wide orange border. After painting the boards white, a border was drawn around the room and masked off with wide masking tape. Another line was measured about 40 cm further in, and masked off. Then fresh orange was painted inside this area, brushing away from the tape to stop any orange bleeding into the white.

Bedlinen: Satin quilts are the new take on the traditional eiderdown. Lighter, sexier and reinvented in the brightest of shades, their satiny good-looks give any bed a glamorous lift. To avoid a clash, team a knock-your-socks-off quilt like this one with white cotton bedding.

The look: This room mixes classic furniture, an old-style, hand-stitched quilt and a cast-iron fireplace with bold walls for a strong, confident look.

Colour: The walls have been painted a striking green. To avoid an almighty colour clash the floor is carpeted in neutral beige and the ceiling is painted white to stop the room feeling small and claustrophobic. A patchwork quilt introduces more colours, but they're faded and soft, to complement, rather than compete with, the walls.

Furniture: To add personality, try using pieces that were not necessarily designed to go in that room. The beautiful old wooden cabinet in this room was probably intended for a kitchen or dining room as a sideboard and display unit, but looks wonderful here, providing storage and shelves for showing off favourite treasures. Its warm golden wood tones in beautifully with an old pine mirror above the fireplace.

Bedlinen: A handmade patchwork quilt adds some softer colour to the room and ensures the bed always looks neat during the day. Splash out on a beautiful quilt like this and you can afford to use less stylish bedlinen beneath, as it will rarely be seen.

The floor: Carpet is kind to bare feet and a neutral tone like this suits most schemes. Here, the same carpet has been laid throughout the upstairs. This is a good way to give your rooms a common theme, creating continuity even when the walls are different shades.

The look: Splashes of clear blue and cool aqua give this bedroom relaxed summer style. Nature is the inspiration for this scheme, creating a laid-back look that's easy to live with.

Colour: The walls are painted a fresh yellowy-green, giving the illusion of sunshine whatever the weather. The walls around the window frame are left white to add contrast and lighten the look, then colourful bedlinen in white, aqua and green is mixed in, creating a really vibrant scheme.

Furniture: For a natural look, choose natural materials. In this room, a bedside unit made from bamboo, and a bedhead made from wood and woven rattan add lots of warmth and texture to the room. It doesn't matter what types of woods or fibres you mix into a room like this – any combination of natural materials will look great.

Bed: Throwing cushions on a bed is the perfect way to work in colour, with the added bonus that you can change them as often as you like – simply rearrange them, re-cover them, or pick up a few new ones. Here, cushions in turquoise and green, made from sensual silk and cool cotton, create mountains of interest and colour, while upping the room's comfort levels, too.

Accessories: A string of pretty lights hung from a corner of the room creates soft, ambient light that's perfect for a relaxing bedroom. Drape them over the headboard or bedside unit for an informal look. Growing plants in a bedroom adds to its natural, fresh look.

The look: Subtle greys, stripes and tactile fabrics create a calm mood in this bedroom. Using pinstripe fabrics here and there gives a grown-up and stylish feel, while the handsome four-poster bed adds a splash of drama and luxury.

Colour: Forget battleship. Grey doesn't have to mean dull and depressing. There's a world of beautiful grey shades out there, from deep slate to soft dove, and this room mixes them together to give a layered, sophisticated look. White walls are the perfect neutral backdrop, and warm wooden furniture varies the colour scheme and gives it depth.

Bed: This is a modern take on the traditional four-poster, with a hint of New England, Ralph Lauren-esque sophistication. To create the ultra-comfortable, relaxing look, it's piled with cushions, pillows and throws in a range of shades and textures. A pinstripe, grey duvet cover provides the base, and cushions with stripe patterns are variations on that theme. A super-tactile suede throw looks and feels gorgeous and shouts grown-up style.

Window: The pinstripe theme is picked up at the window, where a smart Roman blind in soft grey hangs. Stripe fabrics lend themselves to being used for Roman blinds, rather than a straight roller blind, because the deep folds accentuate the vertical pattern.

Accessories: A classic chair with a padded back ups the comfort factor in this room still further. Just don't be tempted to dump clothes on it or you'll hide its soft lines and warm grey upholstery. A bedside lamp with a tall wooden base echoes the long lines of the four-poster, while graphic art in different sizes, hung in a haphazard pattern, adds interest and a hint of contemporary style to the perfectly plain walls.

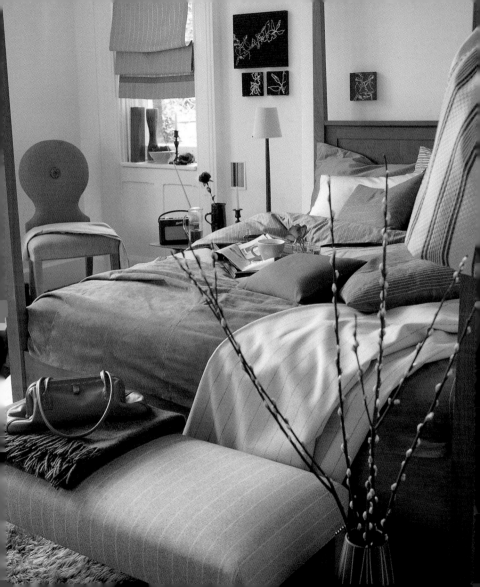

The look: Shimmering satin in a lush pink shade adds a touch of glamour and luxury to this stylish room. Warm colours, natural materials and plenty of cushions beg you to snuggle down, relax and drift off.

Colour: This room shows how a palette of neutral shades – ochre, moss-green, taupe and pale grey – can team beautifully with just one, knock-out bright colour. Here, it's shiny candy-pink, and it gives a modern twist to this laid-back look. A pale grey paint on the walls creates a restrained backdrop for that outspoken pink.

Bed: This bed is upholstered with velvet in a muted, mushroom colour. Its soft lines and smooth texture instantly add a luxurious feel to the room. It has been made up with simple white bedlinen that has a pretty pintuck border design, in a similar shade of mushroom. Added to this are plenty of squishy cushions with beaded and sparkly embroidery that add mountains of style and interest to this room. The pink satin quilt is a show-stopping feature and ups the luxury stakes still further.

Furniture: This room has a laid-back, lived-in look that's ever so elegant. The wardrobe is brand new, but has an aged, mellow look. Rather than a neat, wooden side table with strong lines, there's a raffia table here, rich with texture and softly curved. Instead of pictures on the walls, there are pretty decorative touches, like the Venetian mirror wall sconce and the display shelf, that allows you to change around the objects and images on show whenever you fancy.

The look: This room is inspired by the rich and romantic style of Cuban homes. The ornate stencils, faded paintwork and rich timber furniture of the island's grand old houses meet the more simple, rustic furnishings of local homes.

Colour: Colours are sun-washed and slightly bleached out in Cuban rooms, giving a bright but soft look that's relaxed and lived in, too. Here, the walls are painted in two shades, divided by a stencilled border. Above is a soft, pastel green, and below a golden yellow. The stencil is in a warm teal green and adds energy and elegance to the walls, neatly dividing up the two shades.

Bed: The furniture in this room has a distinctly Spanish flavour to it. A metal bedstead with lots of shapely detail is dressed in lacy bedlinen and draped with filmy white netting. Orange cushions tie in with the yellowy orange on the walls, while white sheets and cushion covers keep the look sunny and fresh.

Window: The window here is enclosed behind shutters, rather than curtains, for a look that's straight from hotter climes. Shutters filter bright sunshine and heat but still let light through. They're found throughout Cuba. Choose white painted shutters, rather than natural wood, for a fresh look.

Accessories: Instead of pictures, the walls are left pretty bare so the stencilling can sing out. A wrought-iron candle sconce looks perfect here. Its curls match those of the bed, and candles provide the kind of soft light a Cuban room might well have relied on.

The look: Bold blue gives a vibrant feel to this little bedroom, reminiscent of sun-baked Mediterranean houses, while chunky old furniture and the odd contemporary piece have the modern day mixing-and-matching style sewn up.

Colour: Blue is generally a cool colour, but darker blues tend to have a much more welcoming, invigorating feel. This shade was inspired by the bold blues painted on houses and window shutters in the Mediterranean. Painting the ceiling and woodwork white ensures that such a strong shade doesn't become overpowering.

Furniture: There's a mix of old and new pieces in this room that works well. An Edwardian wardrobe in rich, dark wood fits perfectly in the alcove to the side of the original chimney breast. A similarly old chair stands by a desk that's bang up-to-date. Designed as a computer desk, with a pull-out shelf for a keyboard, this desk works beautifully here as a sleek, streamlined table or dressing table, its white and metal adding welcome lightness to the room.

Window: Fine, voile curtains instantly give any room a breezy, rather romantic feel. This one has a pretty delphinium design on it, its blue toning in with the walls, making it into a little work of art when drawn across. Voiles are great for hiding nasty views or giving privacy without blocking out precious light – a modern alternative to nets.

Floor: The original Victorian floorboards have been sanded smooth in this room. To create a rich, matt finish like this, try sealing them, then applying floor wax, before buffing off to reveal a warm glow.

The look: With its jewel-bright shades, lengths of sari fabric woven with sparkling gold thread and ornate framed window, this bedroom has a beautiful, Indian feel. This is a confident look that relies on not holding back, so layer the bed with as much colourful bedding as you can, then scatter on richly embroidered and sequined cushions for gorgeous Indian glamour.

Colour: To carry off the Indian look well, be prepared to mix and match lots of hot, bright colour. Fuchsia pink, red, gold and deepest orange clash together beautifully, and shout exotic style.

Walls: With so much colour and vibrancy on the bed, it's a good idea to keep walls soft and subtle. A muted rose pink is used here to create a soothing backdrop, against which the stronger shades sing out. To give these plain walls a strong Indian identity, a length of sari fabric is used to make an eye-catching wall hanging.

Storage: Space under the bed is used as storage but no opportunity to reinforce the Indian look is lost. So instead of plain boxes, here, beaded and jewelled boxes in brightest pink keep bedroom bits and pieces neatly stashed, and are gorgeous enough to be on show.

Window: To give a window an Indian makeover, put up a trellis. This frames the window, changing it from rectangular to curvily arched, a look straight out of a maharajah's palace. Painting it white, tones the trellis in with the rest of the woodwork, its cut-out pattern pretty enough without colour.

The look: This simple, serene scheme has a refreshing, woodland feel. A palette of white and softest green creates a calming atmosphere and makes the most of the natural light that streams in. Simple bedding and furniture add to the restful, unfussy feel.

Colour: Soft green works well in a room that gets a lot of natural light, giving it a sunny, spring-like feel. Too much green can be overwhelming, though, so team it with crisp white to calm it down. Here, white curtains, bedlinen and chest of drawers balance it perfectly. Soft mushroom is the only other shade used in this room. It keeps the mood calm while adding warmth and variety.

Window: This floaty curtain suits the easy, breezy feel of this room. It's made from a length of voile that has been hemmed around the edges and then hung using curtain clips. These clip onto the fabric and can then be threaded onto a curtain wire. Simple.

Furniture: The curvy lines of the wrought-iron bed frame look striking against the green wall and help break it up. They add a little detail and glamour to this very simple scheme, too. A white chest of drawers provides plenty of useful storage and a wicker chair and woven box add some texture.

Bedlinen: Fresh white bedlinen will never go out of style. Invest in good quality white cotton, then splash out on a beautiful coloured quilt or throw to warm it up. If you stick to white bedding, all you have to do is change the throw or scatter over colourful cushions to totally change or update the feel of the room.

The look: There's a colonial, African atmosphere to this bedroom. Sandy shades, shuttered doors and natural materials all contribute, but the look is still fun and eclectic. Rather than sticking religiously to this theme, which can make a room look horribly contrived, here touches of African inspiration are mixed in with more conventional pieces.

Colour: This room has a warm, rich feel to it, provided solely by the furniture and bedlinen, not the walls. These are left pale and neutral, so that the warm wood of the wardrobe and chest of drawers, the artwork and the deep brown quilt take centre stage and work together.

Storage: There's plenty of storage in this good-sized bedroom and it all has a rather traditional feel. An old mirrored wardrobe fits neatly into an alcove, while an equally antique chest of drawers stands alongside. The woods are different shades, but this adds to the warm, vibrant feel in the room. A built-in cupboard has shuttered doors that provide a hint of colonial cool.

Artwork: This huge poster looks dramatic and eye-catching. It's an example of how a bold piece of art can totally redirect the feel of a room. It lends an eclectic vibe to the room and powerfully suggests the African theme, helping to make sense of the other pieces in the room.

Bed: A woven base to the bed and a deep chocolate duvet with a line pattern at the bottom add to the African feel. Those lines could be tall savannah grasses, while the deep brown has an earthy feel that shares the same deep palette as the other pieces in the room.

The look: The bed here is the most dramatic, eye-catching part of this room, with its chunky frame and four-poster feel. The rest of the room has been painted a pale colour and left simple to let this centrepiece stand out.

Bed: If you've got space and want to make a bold statement in your room, invest in a show-stopping bed. This four-poster was made to order by a furniture designer. The headboard is inset with coloured glass and lit from behind, to create a glowing effect. The four posts are gently rounded at the top and three-quarter length height – a modern twist on the traditional, ceiling-height four-poster.

Colour: The pale wooden bed dominates the room and needs a pale background so it can be appreciated. Dramatic furniture like this shouldn't be fighting with a dramatic colour scheme for attention. Floorboards are painted white to match the white walls and ceiling and keep the room light and airy, helping to off-set the heaviness of the bed design.

Bedlinen: Plain white bedlinen looks cool and simple here – perfect on such a bold bed frame. A throw and cushion in soft green add some gentle colour, and a rug on the floor picks up the theme, adding just enough colour to the room to stop it feeling two-tone.

Accessories: A wooden towel rail is a nice addition to this room, standing neatly at the base of the bed, while a wicker laundry basket adds to the room's slightly countrified feel. A few black and white photos complete it – unfussy extras that don't distract from the bed.

The look: A fresh green colour scheme, lots of natural light and a few well-chosen pieces give this room easy-going elegance. To lend it a Christmas flavour, the fireplace has been filled with golden baubles and is flanked by mini firs draped with gold beads.

Colour: Pale green is a spring-like, natural shade that gives this room lots of energy. A few wooden pieces team perfectly with it (think of young trees sprouting bright green leaves and you have your colour combination). A brightly coloured throw picks up on the green theme, blending it with deep blue.

Window: To let maximum light into this spacious room, a simple roller blind has been fitted at the window. Although a big window like this could take heavier curtains, they would decrease the feeling of space and butt up against the neat, streamlined shelves.

Furniture: The room has an original fireplace that gives it real 19th-century charm. A perfect partner is this old cast-iron bed, which oozes character, and is brilliantly teamed up with equally old world pieces: a shapely wooden chair, a carved wooden mirror, and a dark towel rail.

Accessories: Shelves and mantelpiece have been kept reasonably clear in this room, to allow the few ornaments left out to really shine. Rather than displaying objects of different heights, which can create a roller-coaster line around the room, these items are all similar height, for a harmonious effect. If you don't have items that are the same size, try raising one or two on a stack of books, to get a level line.

The look: Rich colours, fat feather eiderdowns and heavy velvet curtains make for a comforting, old-world feel in this room. A big, faded rug softens the wooden boards and adds to the traditional feel.

Colour: This room combines two strong shades: deep red on the curtains and a bluey-green on the walls. Teaming these together gives the room a traditional feel, as modern schemes tend to mix bold colours like red with white or cream. Here, the colours are layered to create a warm, comfortable look. Pinks and reds in the eiderdowns tie in well with the curtains and a chair is covered in green to match the walls.

Curtains: Velvet is great at blocking out light and sound because it's a heavy, thick fabric. Its deep pile does tend to pick up dust, though, so give velvet curtains a good shake out every few months to keep them in top-notch condition.

Wardrobes: The wardrobes are built in and made from rich, golden wood. Getting cupboards made for you is not a cheap option, but it's incredibly space efficient, making excellent use of your room's dimensions and neatly fitting around any tricky angles or features. Built-in storage also helps keep a room clutter-free, as it provides more space than a free-standing wardrobe could.

Bedlinen: Since quilts became the bedding of choice for most of us, traditional sheets, blankets and eiderdowns have lost popularity. But to create a comforting feel, invest in a beautiful warm eiderdown – antique if possible – with a traditional paisley design.

The look: Romantic, peaceful and very, very pretty, this cloudy white haven is the stuff of fairy tales. A frame over the bed is swathed with lengths of white muslin, a super-soft white rug tickles bare toes and palest blue walls add to the clouds and sky scheme.

Bed: The lavish four-poster effect of this bed was easy to pull off. A square frame, the same size as the divan bed, was made from lengths of skirting board fixed together with 5 cm screws. It was then painted white and suspended from the ceiling using cup hooks in each corner and four 50 cm lengths of shiny chain.

Curtains: Muslin curtains were hung around each corner of the suspended frame to create the sense of a four-poster and make the bed feel luxurious and private. They were made with tab tops that can be unbuttoned so it's easy to take the curtains down to wash them. To add interest to the plain muslin, fleur-de-lys patterns were cut from sticky-backed white felt and stuck on at regular intervals.

Colour: This pale scheme layers white on white to create a subtle, floaty feel. The flokati rug adds texture, while the mounds of plain white bedlinen are subtly broken by soft throws in pink and cream. To add definition to the bed, the wall behind is painted grey-blue.

Furniture: This room needs to be clutter-free for the elaborate bed to take centre stage, but the sculpted metal chair, with its curvy, fine lines, looks suitably light and unobtrusive. Painted white, to tie in with the room scheme, it brings a further note of romance to the room.

The look: Thanks to its big bay window, this bedroom gets lots of natural light. The soft colours, big mirror and pale bedlinen maximize this, creating a fresh, airy feel-good atmosphere.

Colour: Colours are bleached out but just strong enough to give the room personality. A serene shade of watery blue and a richer blue carpet provide the soothing base note. Added to it are warm creams, golden wood and a gilt-framed mirror. White curtains and bedding look fresh and unfussy and add to the airy feel.

The bed: This lovely iron bedstead is the focal point. While it would dominate a smaller space, here it looks perfectly at home, its white bedding giving it a light feel, despite its size. With a tall frame there's the advantage of space underneath for storage.

Furniture: There's an informal mix of old and new pieces in this room, adding to its relaxed feel. An old wooden chair with a cane seat sits alongside a padded, cream-upholstered tub chair. A cupboard provides plenty of storage and slots neatly into the alcove by the chimney breast, its soft blue colour helping it blend in with the wall behind.

Window: This bay window has both curtains and blinds at it. A simple roller blind provides privacy at the central pane, while fine curtains hang at either side giving the window shape and interest. The curtains have been made from white cotton, hemmed using iron-on hemming tape, then fixed to the metal rail with clips – a simple and quick method.

TRADITIONAL

The look: Harvest-time colours give this room a sunny, golden, last-days-of-summer feel. An elegant bed makes a stylish centrepiece and a leaf motif is picked up on curtains and chandelier, adding to the room's natural feel.

Colour: The colour scheme is simple and unified in this room. A rich, wheaty shade on the walls, curtains and flooring creates a coordinated base. Added to this is furniture in warm wood. White bedding breaks up the scheme and touches of copper and red are dotted around to draw the eye – the lampshade, the chandelier, the leafy branches by the bed.

Bed: A beautiful, carved bed like this is a real investment. It's not cheap, but its elegant shape is a classic that won't go out of style. It gives the room real personality and makes furnishing it simple. With the bed the centre of attention, the other pieces just need to be simple and solid, in the same warm wood, to complement it.

Window: A length of fabric in a similar tone to the walls hangs from clips attached to a slim rail at the window. If your window isn't that wide, a single curtain is enough, and has a no-fuss, not-too-frilly look that suits today's simple styling. To add a little detail, dried leaves are clipped to the top of the curtain. It's a pretty addition and easy to change, too. Try pinning up feathers, dried flowers, ribbons – whatever takes your fancy.

Chandelier: A sculptural metal chandelier adds the only note of frivolity to this grown-up room. Its curling lines are a welcome contrast to the bed's predominantly straight lines, and the leaf motif ties in with the room's natural look, complementing the leaves on the curtain, too.

The look: This bedroom has a lovely light feel, thanks to its huge window. The most is made of all that natural light through the decor and furniture – creamy walls that are warm and sunny, an elegant white wrought-iron bed and plenty of colourful bedding in welcoming natural tones.

Colour: Pale colours on the walls suit a light-flooded room like this, enhancing the brightness and giving the space a fresh, open feel. Here, creamy walls are teamed with a pale floor for a simple, neutral backdrop. A wrought-iron bed is big, but doesn't dominate thanks to its white frame. A storage box, also in white, ties in with the scheme perfectly.

Bed: A wrought-iron bed makes a big statement in a bedroom, but its size and shape is instantly softened if the frame is painted white. White also gives a classic bed like this a contemporary touch. Layered bedding in a mix of white and earthy berry tones softens the look further. Iron bedsteads are also perfect for hanging things off. Resist the urge just to dump your clothes here and use the end posts to display pretty bags or scarves instead.

Storage: In a big bedroom, the space at the end of the bed is an ideal spot for a chest or blanket box. They look surprisingly unobtrusive when positioned here and provide acres of useful storage. Keep out-of-season clothes or blankets and duvets in here. They can absorb so much stuff that you may find you can get away with a smaller wardrobe.

The look: This bedroom oozes tranquility and elegance, which is impressive since it also serves as a small home office. Shapely furniture and a decorative screen keep desk space out of sight, so the room has a restful, relaxing feel when work is done.

Colour: Lavender is a perfect colour for a bedroom because it's very relaxing and calming. This strong, rich shade works beautifully with cream, rather than white, which would be too stark to complement such a warm colour. Here, cream crops up on the furniture, blinds and carpet, helping to keep the room looking light. To define the working area, the alcove has been painted a soft grey.

The alcove: Alcoves at the side of an old chimney breast lend themselves to being converted into workspace. Here, floating shelves that have no visible brackets provide neat storage for files and papers while a small desk slots underneath without eating into the room. The elegant French-style screen hides the office corner from view in an instant when it comes to bedtime.

Window: Bay windows can be tricky to dress, but here, custom-made Roman blinds that fit each of the three sides of the window look neat, unfussy and stylish. In neutral linen, each blind is heavily lined to help keep out the light and muffle traffic noise from the busy road below.

Furniture: There's a romantic feel to the pieces in this bedroom. The shapely wrought-iron bed is painted cream to give it a soft look, while both the chest of drawers and bedside table have the curvy lines of antique French pieces. Again, by simply painting them cream they look classic and timeless.

The look: This ultra-feminine bedroom has a beautiful mix of characterful furniture, mirrors, lighting and colour. There's lots to draw the eye and plenty of pretty details, but the room still has a breezy, uncluttered feel.

Colour: The walls have been painted a soft shade of purplish blue to create a colourful but subtle backdrop. A patchwork quilt with lots of pink, lilac and white mixed in adds more gentle colour and plenty of cushions, flowers and pots in similar girlie shades add to the soft, welcoming feel.

Lighting: There's a mix of lighting in this room. An elegant chandelier creates a dramatic focal point, while a feathery lamp in candy pink adds a fun, contemporary feel. A string of tiny fairy lights draped over the mirror look lovely when switched on. As the bedroom is one room you always spend time in at night, it's a good idea to work in a couple of light sources, so you can tailor the light levels to your needs. Ambient light, like these fairy lights, is no good for reading by, but it can really add to the mood of the room, creating a peaceful, warm atmosphere.

Accessories: Mirrors in a bedroom are both practical and decorative and help to increase the feeling of light and space. Here, a large, square mirror with a metal frame fills a whole wall, while a smaller, more decorative oval mirror is hung above the dressing table where it's used for putting on makeup. Favourite photos, pots and girlie accessories, like a feather-trimmed brush pot, give this room bags of character and a friendly, informal feel, and while there is plenty on show, it's a carefully controlled mix, so the room doesn't feel cluttered or untidy. Cosmetics, bottles and bits are stored out of sight.

The look: Bold, Mediterranean colours and warm, aged wood combine beautifully in this bedroom to create a welcoming feel. A ceiling beam has been left exposed and window and door frames preserved in their original bare wood state, rather than painted, to add to the charm-filled rustic feel.

Colour: The colourful, checked bedspread is the eye-catching focus of this room, with its rich oranges, yellows and green. Curtains and cushions in similar shades continue the colourful theme, but to prevent the room having a too neat, over-coordinated feel, fabrics with different patterns have been used for each. Both lampshades are less zingy than the other soft furnishings, but still echo the chequer-board theme that runs through all the soft furnishing materials.

Walls: Walls are simply painted in white to create a neutral backdrop that helps keep the room feeling fresh. To add interest, a delicate leaf pattern has been stencilled around the eaves in soft ochre shades. Pick up a stencilling kit from any art or craft shop but, if you've never tried stencilling before, experiment first on a section of wall that can't be seen – behind a wardrobe or bed, for example.

Floor: These original wooden floorboards add a rich brown that anchors the whole look. They have been cleaned up with bleach, to remove dirt and paint, then coated with floor polish to give a matt protective finish. If you prefer boards with a shinier finish, try using varnish instead.

The look: Peaceful, restful and elegant, this is country style with an up-to-date edge. Furniture is shapely and sensual, colours are designed to help you relax and a feather motif on the wall adds just the right amount of detail to this simple, relaxed room.

Colour: Lilac is one of the most peaceful, soothing shades in the spectrum – perfect for a bedroom. Teamed with white it looks fresh and stylish, while splashes of turquoise on the bed add a necessary hint of dark colour that stops the scheme from looking washed out.

Bed: This wrought-iron double bedstead is pure country style at its most romantic. Its sensual curves and delicate detailing give it grace and femininity – just right for a peaceful room like this. To let its curvy lines take centre stage, it's dressed simply in a lilac duvet with just a couple of cushions scattered over to break up the colour.

Walls: A soft, lilac shade is painted onto the walls, creating a relaxed backdrop without being obtrusive. To add interest, a tall feather design has been stencilled onto the wall in white paint. It's an original alternative to hanging pictures and its delicate lines suit the room's airy feel. A design like this is versatile, too – when you get bored of it and want to try something new, just paint straight over it.

Window: For the bed to be the focal point of this room, the window treatment has to be simple and sleek. A roller blind in white fabric is the perfect solution. It's modern and unfussy and doesn't pull attention away from the real heart of this room.

The look: The owners of this fresh lemon bedroom chose bright and sunny colours because they wanted a happy start to the day. Matching green bedding and curtains with a cheery, flower design complete the room and pine furniture adds a warm note of country style.

Colour: Lemon yellow will make even the darkest room feel brighter, but in a bedroom like this, blessed with plenty of natural light, it creates a powerfully sunny feel. Lime greens and powdery blues coordinate well with it, for a no-holds-barred colourful look.

Furniture: A big pine bed takes centre stage in this bedroom. Warm-looking and reassuringly chunky, it gives the room an unpretentious feel and shouts comfort. A matching mirror unit, perched on the windowsill, has the same curvy lines and rich tones, for a coordinated, country look.

Bedlinen and curtains: If you want a room to look simple and thoroughly coordinated, go for matching curtains and bedlinen. Here, a fabric with a contemporary flower design adds to the friendly county look, while keeping the room feeling up-to-date. Using the same fabric throughout suits a small room; too many different patterns can make it feel crowded. If you like this neatly matching look, it's a good idea to buy a spare set of bedlinen in the same design or the effect will be lost when you change the sheets.

The look: If your taste leans towards relaxed country style, but you're not wild about the floral prints that so often feature in it, try this modern take on a rustic look. Classic country ingredients like pale painted floorboards and an old iron bed frame get a contemporary rethink here with vibrant, stripy bedlinen.

Colour: If you want to have a bright duvet cover like this one, you can't afford to have bright walls too (unless you like a headache every morning when you wake up). Here, the candy stripe shades can sing out because they're set against a neutral backdrop of white walls, cream floorboards and untreated wooden furniture.

Bed: This old bed frame oozes character. Its traditional shape and slightly beaten up look give it bags of country-style cool. You can find beds like this in second-hand stores and markets, then just buy a new mattress – the result is a bed with old rustic style and up-to-date comfort. A little step stool next to it makes a perfect bedside table. The untreated wood adds to the relaxed look, but a lick of white or cream paint would look equally good.

Bedlinen: Colourful stripes look super-stylish and give this bed a fresh look. Using bright bedlinen is a much easier way of introducing colour into a bedroom than painting the walls a bold shade. When you tire of the pattern or shades, all you have to do is change the sheets – simple. If you get sick of the colour on your walls, you have to re-paint your whole room – not quite so simple.

The look: Bright white and soft stripes make for a refreshing bedroom retreat. Shades of blue and aqua create a seaside feel, while rustic furniture completes the relaxed look.

Colour: White is the base colour in this room – a shade that introduces a fresh, summery feel. Its partner is blue, mixed into mostly striped fabric for a New England beach house scheme. An easy way to create a strong but interesting scheme is to mix two colours – here white and blue – but add variety by choosing colours of every shade and depth, from navy to watery pastels.

Bed: To create the perfect private place for a snooze, this bed has a curtain hung at one end that can be pulled across. The bed is piled high with cushions and pillows in a mix of patterns and shades for maximum comfort – a look like this doesn't need neatly coordinating patterns.

Floor: Pale floorboards make a nice, light base and suit this room's fresh feel. A small blue rug adds comfort and more colour. Try laying a rug at an angle, as here – it gives a relaxed, informal feel to a room.

Furniture: A couple of stools have been used to great effect here. A small wooden stool is painted blue and serves as a handy bedside table while a white step stool is the perfect place for displaying plants. It's always worth looking out for simple furniture in untreated wood. It's inexpensive, and with a lick of paint you can give it a fresh look that will perfectly fit in with your chosen room colour scheme.

The look: A combination of pastel shades can look sugary and cloying, but here only the palest and most airy colours are used to create a room that's fresh, feminine and bursting with spring.

Walls: A mixture of panelling and wallpaper gives these walls bags of style. Tongue-and-groove panelling, painted white and running around the room at half height, creates a country feel. Its wide top also provides a place to display favourite pieces. The wallpaper is in palest pastel pink, with a trellis-work pattern of pale green leaves and blowzy blue flowers. It's pretty, subtle and very feminine, nicely balanced by the no-fuss panelling.

Bed: Pale wood and frosted glass are key to this room's airy look. A frosted glass headboard looks modern without jarring with the room's elegant feel. Crisp white bedlinen adds a light, classic feel, while a soft blue blanket tones in well with the flowers in the wallpaper.

Furniture: Pale, honey-coloured wood suits a light, girlie room like this. Dark wood would ruin the spring-like feel. A chest of drawers and neat little side table in warm maple are matched by the wood of the lamp and bed frame.

Accessories: A feminine room like this is crying out for pretty things to be dotted around. Pictures are lined up on top of the panelling, hooks and a pretty frame sit on the bedside table and hanging from the chest of drawers is a drawstring laundry bag, perfect for storing underwear, socks and scarves.

The look: Flourishes of wrought-iron add a decorative edge to this peaceful, cream bedroom. A limed pine chest and mirror add a relaxed, aged feel to the room, while perfectly coordinating with its cool, light-filled feel.

Bed: This wrought-iron bed frame has a few decorative curls, so it looks elegant, but not fussy. Its strong lines look perfect against the cream walls, creating a dramatic outline. Cream bedlinen with a subtle stripe looks stylish and understated and a creamy cushion with a ridged cover adds a touch of texture.

Furniture: The chest of drawers and mirror are both made from reclaimed pine that has been limed with wax to give it a pale, distressed finish. Black wrought-iron handles fitted to the drawers are the perfect finishing touch. In keeping with the iron theme, the lamp has a curly base and there's a candle sconce above the bed, too.

Window: Lightweight creamy curtains hang at this window, pulled back in a generous sweep and secured with a rope and wrought-iron tie-back. The room's two themes – cream and wrought-iron – are beautifully combined here, creating a well thought-out, effortlessly coordinated look.

Accessories: This room's restful feel is owed to the absence of colour and elaborate details, so accessories have been kept to a minimum. Deep drawers provide useful storage, leaving the top of the chest home only to a clock and a couple of favourite pieces, both in cream, to suit the room.

The look: There's a fresh and relaxing feel to this room, perfect for unwinding in and drifting off to sleep. Lilac walls, lots of cushions and a pretty bedspread in a floral pattern give the room an airy look that's easy to live with.

Colour: Lilac relaxes and soothes, so it's ideal for a bedroom. Here, lilac-painted walls are complemented by an old quilt with a lilac centre and paisley border. Cushions and blankets are in deeper purple and pink shades, adding depth and vibrant detail to this quiet, mellow room.

Bedlinen: An old quilt gives the iron bed a touch of country chic. Its colours tone in perfectly with the wall, while its soft pattern adds a bit of interest and warmth. Don't be afraid to mix and match patterns with a quilt like this. Scatter over pretty cushions in lively colours for a comfy, laid-back look.

Storage: A bedside table that also has drawer space is an invaluable addition to any bedroom. There's further storage at the foot of the bed – an often wasted space – in the shape of a large wicker basket, which is a handy place for keeping bedlinen.

Screens: There are two decorative screens in this room. The metal screen behind the bed is part of a garden furniture range, with muslin panels added to soften its look. A wooden screen in the opposite corner is painted with a delicate lily design, so it looks beautiful, but is useful, too. Use it to hide an ugly corner or a pile of boxes.

The look: This simple, stylish bedroom is elegance personified. There are no ornate details, no bright, jarring colours or busy artwork, just cool colours and lots of light.

Colour: Pale blue walls contrast with the white bedlinen to create a soothing atmosphere in this room. Blue and white are the chief colours in the room with touches of black or dark brown the only other shades, and this simplicity is key to its success. The pale blue also changes with the light and adds subtle interest to this small space.

Bed: A simple wrought-iron bedstead adds graphic shape to the room and its headboard stands out beautifully against the cool walls. White bedding looks light and fresh and will never date, while an intricately jewelled cushion injects just the right amount of pattern into the scheme.

Window: Simple elegance is what this room is all about so busy curtains wouldn't work here. Instead, a slick roller blind in white fabric looks perfect and can be adjusted to any height to help soften the bright sunlight that floods in.

Accessories: Lots of extras would spoil the peace and calm of this room, so accessories have been kept to a tasteful minimum. A shapely bundle of sticks adds delicate interest in the corner, while a wreath of twigs on the wall echoes the circular design of the bed. An old Bakelite telephone looks handsome and stylish, and pretty white flowers complete the look and match the colour scheme perfectly.

The look: Soft white and simple furnishings give this room a light, sunny feel that's certain to make you relax.

Colour: White is a sure-fire way to keep a room feeling light, but there are two families of white to choose from: those with yellow or earthy undertones, and those with blue or grey undertones. In a sunny room, you can afford to use either – here, a soft, warm white has been used to maximize the light. In a dark room, steer clear of whites with grey or blue in them as they can look cold.

Floor: The all-white theme could have been continued onto the floorboards – white painted boards help bounce light around – but it would have made the room too pale.

Instead, natural wood boards with a rich, matt brown finish add warmth and team perfectly with the snowy scheme.

Furniture: An old Lloyd Loom chair and a big, woven chest are a couple of the rustic ingredients in this room. Slightly battered looking and full of character, they're also both incredibly useful, performing a practical role in the room, as well as a decorative one.

Bed: Crisp white bedlinen with a touch of red in it brings a welcome shot of colour to the room. The iron bed frame is also the perfect place to hang clothes or bags from. A pretty blouse like this looks like a little artwork, hung here, and adds some welcome colour to the pale scheme.

The look: Relaxed, elegant and full of country romance, this room has a comfortable, restful feel that's perfect for a bedroom. Mounds of pretty, faded floral quilts and crisp white bedding invite you to snuggle up while soft lilac walls create a peaceful backdrop that will lull you to sleep.

Colour: Faded pastel shades are central to country style, a look that's understated and lived in. Here, the muted lilac of the walls is picked up in the flowers on the quilts and curtains. A woven rug tones in with the bare boards and its lilac border matches the walls and bedding for a loosely coordinated look.

Furniture: This wrought-iron bed is painted cream to soften its appearance. Next to it is a distressed wooden table, its pale paint chipped over years of use, giving the room an air of simple, rustic elegance. A shelf underneath provides room for books, while space under the bed has been maximized with an old suitcase and floral box – both look great, while creating extra storage.

Bedlinen: Faded floral quilts shout country style. Don't be afraid to mix and match patterns, just layer them on for a comfy, higgledy-piggledy look – country style is not about being precise. A variety of floral patterns will look great side-by-side, so long as they are roughly the same shade – a really bright quilt here would jar and spoil the effect.

Accessories: A little display of paintings looks lovely above the bed, and its grouping is pleasingly off-centre – another way to create a laid-back look. Fabric butterflies tied to the headboard and a window box crammed with flowers add fun and colour.

The look: There's an all-out nautical theme to this nursery. Sea-green walls, a sailing ship border and curtains, and a liner-shaped bookcase combine for a fun, engaging room with lots to amuse and inspire young minds.

Colour: Turquoise on the walls sets the seaside theme and it's a unisex colour that will appeal to both girls and boys. If you have two children of different sexes who need to share a room, it's important to choose a shade that both will enjoy. All the woodwork has been painted white to brighten the room. To give the look a strong identity, more blues have been mixed in, but very few other colours.

Wall: To break up the turquoise paint and add some fun detail, a ship design border is pasted on. A large radiator under the window is disguised with a fretwork cover, painted white so it looks fresh and bright.

Window: There's more nautical action at the window, with curtains made from a ship-design fabric. The curtain pole is painted the same shade of blue as the walls, so it blends in, and a blue tie-back shaped like a sea horse is fixed to the wall, injecting yet more seaside fun and allowing the curtains to be pulled well clear of the window, letting in the maximum amount of light.

Bed: A plain bed has been painted white, then an octopus design has been painted onto the headboard. The stripy bedding is actually a plain duvet set with lengths of ribbon and mirror discs stitched on to create a cheerful nautical stripe and porthole design.

The look: There's a fresh, colourful, Scandinavian theme to this child's bedroom. Wooden furniture, painted for a folksy feel, wooden flooring and plenty of clean, bright colours are the key ingredients, blended together for an easy-to-live-with and calm effect.

Colour: White should be the base colour of any Scandinavian scheme, then just add clean, strong, simple shades like red, blue or lilac. Here, white walls are broken up with a run of wood panelling painted a softer cream. Pale wooden flooring complements, then dashes of rich red are added on curtains, furniture, bedding and rugs.

Window: An unfussy window treatment helps keep this look relaxed and breezy. A slightly sheer red-and-white check fabric has been hung simply at the window. If the room is very bright, try teaming this with a heavier linen roller blind that will block out morning rays.

Furniture: Wooden furniture is at the heart of the Scandinavian look, and here, a white painted cot is teamed with a red chair, decorated along its back for a folksy feel. The plain cot is softened and given life by adding patchwork quilts and a pretty blue and white pillowcase.

Floor: Scandinavian floors are generally wooden, which is clean, hygienic and easy to care for. A scrubbed or limewashed finish is the best choice, as it looks relaxed and lived in. To soften bare boards, add rag or cotton rugs or mats for a hint of colour at floor level and a soft surface for young knees and hands.

The look: This room has four looks in one. It has been divided into different areas and painted to represent the four elements: earth, water, air and fire. It's a colourful scheme with lots to interest and amuse children.

Earth area: Strong green and a leaf motif have been used. The deep green fabric bedcovers and headboard are made from white cotton canvas, dyed with a leaf-print design using light-activated dye. The fabric was dampened and painted with a solution of two-parts water, one-part dye. Leaves were then laid on top before it dried. When the canvas was left in the sun, the light reacted with the dye, colouring exposed areas green. Plasterboard pinboards above both beds have been painted pale green and stamped with images of trees.

Water area: A sea theme has been created by painting the wall a sea-blue and decorating it with paper fish, painted orange and silver using artist's acrylics. The bubbles have been painted on with silver spray-paint. A set of shelves fixed above has been painted in similar shades of aqua to match the paintwork.

Air area: The window is the natural place to decorate with the air theme. Here, walls and the edges of the window frames are bright sky-blue and fluffy clouds have been stencilled on in white. A chest of drawers has been painted the same way.

Fire area: (Not visible in picture.) Bright yellow walls create a fiery look, and flame stencils have been added to complete it. To stop the colour dominating that wall, it has only been painted part way up, with white above to soften it.

The look: There's a fun, nautical feel to this children's bedroom, with plenty of seaside accessories and bold navy and white bedding. A bunk bed makes economical use of the space, providing room for two children to sleep and leaving floor space free for them to play or read on.

Colours: It's often tempting to use bold, cheery colours in a child's bedroom, but this room illustrates how a traditionally adult scheme of cream and navy can suit a young person's room beautifully and help it to feel fresh, spacious and inviting. Barley-white on the walls and the bed's woodwork is teamed with a warmer, honey-coloured carpet. This is practical, too. A paler carpet would show dirt too easily to suit a child's room.

Furniture: Although the bunk bed takes up most of the room, it's also part of it, because it's built in, and so gives the room its identity. Panelling on the bed frame is also used on the walls, helping it blend in, and a sturdy fixed ladder means it's super-safe, too. In a small room, furniture needs to work extra hard to earn its space, so the old traveller's trunk does two jobs – it's both storage and a surface for drawing or working on.

Accessories: Although the room has a grown-up colour scheme, the nautical bits and bobs give it a sense of childish fun and spirit. Carved boats and colour postcards on the wall, a ship's wheel propped against a wall and a lighthouse on the chest give the room plenty of personality.

The look: A bold turquoise colour scheme gives this bright, sun-drenched bedroom bags of character. It's cosy without being twee or girlie, bright without being obvious and primary coloured and stylish without being precious.

Walls: To make this room as practical as possible, while keeping it fun and toddler-friendly, the lower half of the walls are covered with tongue-and-groove panelling, painted with a tough oil-based paint. This panelling also has the added benefit of hiding any imperfections in the plasterwork. The dado rail is interspersed with rows of pegs for hanging bags, clothes and odds and ends. It also creates a small ledge on which pictures can be propped.

Colour: Turquoise on the walls is a bold choice, but the room gets lots of light so can carry it off. To tone it down, there's a silver-grey carpet, off-white painted furniture and pretty check blinds in cream and blue.

Windows: The blinds have been made from a texture-rich blanket fabric to cosy-up the room and backed with plain cotton fabric to shut out as much light as possible – crucial for a room in which a toddler will be taking plenty of daytime naps.

Furniture: A solid wooden bed painted an off-white takes pride of place and is the kind of classic design that a child can grow up with. Child-friendly pieces are dotted around, giving the room a sense of identity and fun. There's a scaled-down version of an adult dining chair, and lots of baskets and boxes for toys.

The look: This colourful baby's room has vibrant walls, a chunky, bespoke cot and a fun dinosaur theme running through it. The colours are warm, the patterns bold and the overall feel inviting, happy and comfortable.

Walls: The dinosaur border was picked for the room first, providing a ready-made colour scheme of yellow and orange. A green and yellow checked wallpaper has been pasted around the lower part of the room, while above the border a sunshiny orange paint adds warmth and zing. The finishing touch is a cute hand-painted dinosaur on the wall above the cot – something for baby to stare up at.

Window: Simple curtains in the same vibrant shades of orange and yellow hang at the window and are pinned back by day with a pair of chunky dinosaur tie-backs. These were made using off-cuts of MDF, cut to shape then painted yellow. A yellow roller blind has been hung, too, so the room can be darkened thoroughly when the baby is napping during the day and at night.

Furniture: This striking cot has been handmade so it is unique and eye-catching. The wood has been treated to a purple stain so it stands out against the hot wall colours. Bedlinen in a matching lavender has a detail of yellow flowers, so it ties in prettily with the walls. The floor is kept uncluttered so there's space for a soft mat for the baby to lie and play on.

The look: This child's bedroom has heaps of toys and books to hand, but still manages to look serene and stylish. A wall of shelves provides storage while comfy floor cushions offer a place to curl up and read.

Colour: This room uses pale colours to create an airy, peaceful feel. Limestone-coloured walls are complemented by a rich, elm wood floor. A dark red throw adds the one deep colour. Soft blue and white are the only other shades used.

Bed: A simple bed is transformed into the perfect little hideaway with a pullback curtain around it. Simply fix an MDF pelmet between two walls and hang a high-tension curtain wire behind to suspend a ready-made curtain.

Furniture: Create a chill-out zone in your child's room with beanbags and floor cushions, such as this versatile stripy cube. Shelves make the perfect

place to clip on a reading light. You can also keep a light for use at night on here. This pierced ceramic light, used with a night light bulb, will create a soft reassuring glow.

Storage: Children's rooms always need plenty of storage to keep toys, pens and books neatly stashed. Here, two short and one long shelf, positioned high enough to be out of a toddler's reach, store most bits and bobs. A basket on the top is home to smaller items, while larger pieces look great displayed alone. Drawers under the bed create even more hideaway space.

The look: This cheery, welcoming bedroom is the kind of space that a child can grow up into. A won't-date colour scheme that's not too babyish, and plenty of space for a desk and personal objects, mean it could keep a young person (and their parents) happy for years.

Colour: Orange and yellow always look cheerful and sunny. Here, checked bedding and curtains marry both shades, but are made from different fabrics, stopping the room from looking overly coordinated. Walls are painted a soft cream up to the picture rail, then white above and across the ceiling, to add a sense of height and space to the room.

Furniture: All the pieces in this room look comfortably old – the wicker chest, the desk and rattan-seated chair – giving the room character and warmth. The bed has a plain white valance around it – a great way to hide the often hectic patterns you find on divan bases, plus it keeps the room looking fresh and neat.

Accessories: Instead of artwork on the walls, a pinboard hangs from the picture rail, smothered with photos, school certificates and pictures – all things that are more meaningful to a child than a framed picture would be. In a fairly small room like this, it helps to keep floor space clear, so the room feels as big as possible, and one trick is to use your walls. Here, clever use has been made of two Shaker-style peg rails. They're not home to clothes or coats, but to teddies, hats and puppets.

The look: Who says nurseries have to be painted in soft, peaceful shades? This room shows how strong colour can create mountains of interest in a child's room, without the need for fussy accessories.

Colour: Every surface is bright and bold in this room, and strong shade has been teamed with strong shade to great effect. One red wall, one blue and a green carpet sit happily alongside each other, and rather than the usual white, the ceiling has been painted a sunny yellow. The same yellow has been used on the skirting boards and window frame, so that, even though there are lots of different shades here, they're all pulled together.

Floor: Children use the floor for playing, sitting and crawling, so carpet is ideal in a child's room because it's soft and warm. This one is in a rich green that will hide dirt and add more colour to this bold room. A neutral carpet could have looked lost here. In a kid's room, where spills and marks are inevitable, it's a good idea to have carpet Scotchgarded to protect it.

Bedlinen: The colourful cot duvet set was the inspiration for this room's colour scheme. Often, people match their bedding to their wall colour, but it's just as effective to work the other way round. If you fall in love with a colourful bedspread, why not use it as the basis for a room's look?

Furniture: There's minimal furniture in this nursery. Until children get older, when they need toys around them, their bedrooms can afford to be pared down. A handsome wooden cot and a cute Mickey Mouse painting are the sole ingredients, but the room doesn't feel bare thanks to all that vibrant colour.

CHILDREN'S

The look: This bedroom is home to two young children so needs to be multi-functional. Colours are kept deliberately simple, letting the details do the rest, and plenty of cunning storage ideas have been mixed in to make use of every spare centimetre of space.

Colour: The walls are painted in a soft green colour with a lime hint. Green is a versatile shade that works well with neutrals, pastels and vibrant shades. The ceiling is painted a clean white to keep the room simple and fresh, while curtains with a soft brush stroke design add a splash of detail. The rest of the colour is supplied via the kids' things – bright toys, teddies and pictures.

Bed: A bunk bed is the obvious choice for a bedroom that's home to more than one child. You can make it even more practical and space-saving by storing toys in boxes underneath and fixing fabric storage pockets and panels over the frame. Make them from a strong fabric, hemmed around the edges, then fix to the frame with Velcro.

Lighting: The bottom bed of a bunk can be dark, but here two lamps are wall-mounted above each pillow to provide light for kids to read by. They can turn them off or on when it suits, without disturbing the other child or blinding them with an overhead light.

Desk and chair: Kids need a place to do homework, draw or read in a bedroom, so a desk and chair is essential. In this room, where space is short, a folding desk and chair are perfect. Fit hooks to the wall then just hang them out of the way when you need to free up floor space for play.

The look: Fresh blues, lots of silvery-grey woodwork and an indoor climbing wall provide plenty to exercise a young mind and body. The scheme is fun and refreshing without being childish. This is a room that a child can enjoy well into adolescence.

Colour: The walls have been painted three different but complementary shades. A soft Wedgwood blue, a turquoise green and a bright greeny-blue look great side by side and add a fun, youthful feel to the room. The wardrobe and bunk bed are painted a very pale shade of lavender-grey satin wood that tones in nicely with the blue and green scheme.

Climbing wall: This climbing wall must be on every boy's wish list. It's made from professional climbing holds screwed into sturdy 18 mm plywood that is then fixed to the wall. A coat of paint and varnish protects the wood and lets it fit in with the rest of the scheme.

Noticeboard: A noticeboard is great for keeping a child's room organized. This is made from a piece of 12 mm plywood covered with a layer of wadding and felt, and finished off with criss-cross ribbons secured with drawing pins.

Storage: Shelves fit perfectly in this room's alcove and provide acres of useful storage. To keep things even tidier, store toys in labelled tins that can sit neatly on the shelves or under the bed. In a good-sized room like this, a big wardrobe fits in perfectly without dominating. This one has heaps of hanging space as well as a deep drawer.

The look: There's a pretty, Scandinavian theme to this toddler's bedroom. A fun, white-painted sleigh bed takes centre stage with gingham curtains in soft lilac at the window and lots of subtle purples, mauves and greys mixed in. It's a classic, jolly style that a child (or you) won't tire of quickly.

Colour: The traditional baby pinks, blues and yellows so often seen in children's rooms can look cloying and soon seem grubby and tired. So instead, this bedroom has a soothing scheme of pale grey, purple and mauve, set off with a warm, heather-coloured carpet and an off-white paint on the walls. It's a scheme that any child would be happy to grow up into.

Window: This bedroom gets lots of natural light, so to make the most of it and keep the room feeling sunny, semi-sheer purple and white curtains were hung at the window, in front of a linen blind that keeps the sunlight out in the bright early mornings of summer.

Bed: This mini sleigh bed is a fun addition to a child's room. Painted white, it is bursting with Scandinavian style. Adding lots of cushions and soft blankets make it a cosy nest for reading and playing, as well as sleeping.

Walls: Walls are painted a soft, off-white so the room feels light and won't date. A white peg rail turns an empty wall into extra storage space – plus it looks pretty, too. Pictures are then perched on top, secured to the wall with a mirror plate or glue gun, so little hands can't yank them off.

The look: Fresh and inviting, this bathroom combines white mosaic tiles, a white suite and an attractive mix of plants and pictures to give the room bags of personality and style. Pretty bottles of bath products look attractive and add a touch of spa-like luxury.

Colour: White is guaranteed to give a bathroom a fresh, clean feel. Here, a white suite, tiles and towels are teamed with neutral flooring. Warmth is injected with a row of framed pictures, rustic storage pots and mounds of Mind Your Own Business, growing in mesh containers.

Suite: The bath taps are wall-mounted and positioned in the centre of the bath, leaving each curved end free for lying back and relaxing. A modern, slim showerhead is also wall-mounted so it can be stored neatly out of the way.

Accessories: White towels suit any bathroom – they're classic, versatile and also very practical. You can keep adding to your collection or replacing them from any store, without having to worry about getting a matching shade or buying them from a specific place. Only the best bath products are left out in this room to maintain its luxury feel. Less glamorous bottles are stored out of sight.

Tiles: White mosaic tiles make a watertight splashback by the bath and are continued up across the shelf and onto the wall to protect all surfaces from splashes. Although they look fiddly, mosaics are generally sold attached to square meshes, so they're surprisingly easy and quick to lay.

The look: White blossoms standing out against a deep blue sky are the inspiration for this room, echoed in the fresh white fittings and intense azure walls. Texture is added with the soft green mosaic-look flooring and a woven basket or two, while depth and warmth comes from the dark brown shelf and storage cupboard.

Colour: All the colours are clear and strong in this show-stopping modern bathroom. Intense azure-blue gives the walls knockout boldness, while a bright white suite stands out clearly against it. Darker tones are added with a wooden drawer unit and dark wooden shelf, and dashes of deep green crop up elsewhere on glass accessories and tiles.

Furniture: Rather than a wall unit, there's a free-standing cupboard on the floor of this room. Its dark wood matches the shelf and its woven drawers add natural texture and tie in with the baskets. In a spacious bathroom like this, free-standing pieces are ideal and can be moved around as you like. An old garden chair adds a final dose of laid back charm to the room and calls to mind the outdoors, just as the colour scheme does.

Suite: The clean lines of this white bathroom suite are simplicity itself. Shiny chrome mixer taps with a contemporary shape add more modern glamour, with the bathroom taps mounted in the middle of the bath to allow you to lie comfortably at either end.

Floor: This floor is a great example of how versatile vinyl is. It comes in so many designs and colours, many of which mimic the effect of natural stone or slate flooring, without its price or disadvantages (stone and slate can be cold and hard underfoot).

The look: This bathroom has lots of modern touches – wall-mounted taps, a vast fitted mirror, mosaic tiling – yet its overall look is one of airy elegance that is timeless. Fitted cupboards keep bits and pieces out of sight, creating a clutter-free, relaxing space.

Colour: Although there is colour in this room, it's carefully chosen to be subtle and peaceful. Mosaics in soft, watery blue team beautifully with a white suite, white cupboards and ceiling. The laminate floor is in an equally pale shade and tones in with the woven laundry basket and wooden bath rack.

Suite: A big, broad basin would crowd out a small bathroom, but this bathroom is a good size so it can take it. Fitting wall-mounted taps keeps its strong shape uninterrupted. There are lots of basins on the market that don't have the traditional pedestal, but are simply wall-mounted, like this one. They can help make the room feel bigger, because you can see all the wall space beneath the basin. By contrast, the bath can be far less eye-catching in design because it's almost completely hidden behind a tiled panel.

Tiles: The lofty dimensions of this room mean that, when tiling up to the ceiling, it's essential to choose tiles that aren't too overbearing because you're going to see a lot of them. Using white grout with these pale blue mosaics keeps them looking fresh, but remember that coloured grouts are available and suit some schemes beautifully.

Mirror: Covering part of one wall with a mirror not only looks dramatic, it helps keep the room bright by bouncing light around it. Here, a false wall conceals all the basin's pipework and the mirror sits perfectly in the recess created by it.

CONTEMPORARY

The look: This smart shower room mixes the latest chic bathroom fittings with pieces that have lots of personality to create a softly modern feel. A big window keeps the room bright, helped along by an all-white scheme.

Colour: There's very little colour in this room, which is why it feels so clean and light – ideal for a bathroom. White walls, white mosaic tiles in the shower and a pale carpet are the key ingredients. There's plenty of light-reflecting chrome, too, plus a huge mirror that bounces daylight around the room to great effect.

Suite: A free-standing basin like this is a modern classic. Here, old reclaimed floorboards have been turned into a table to support it, then treated with yacht varnish to make them waterproof. Wall-mounted taps help show off the basin's smooth lines.

Shower: This walk-in unit has a power shower. Power showers have a pump built in that forces water out at high pressure so they only work with certain types of water systems. If you have a combination boiler that heats water on demand, you can't have a power shower, as the boiler can't heat the water fast enough to cope with the rapid water flow.

Accessories: As it's a good size, there's space in this bathroom for a few characterful bits and pieces. A soft armchair in palest grey adds comfort, while a small fold-up table looks sweet and is a useful perch for books or cups. A wooden box beneath the basin provides storage for bathroom bits, leaving surfaces clear so the room feels uncluttered.

The look: Despite having no window, this bathroom has a deliciously light and airy feel. The style is simple and practical, with a contemporary twist, thanks to the modern suite and up-to-date materials.

Colour: An all-white scheme suits a windowless bathroom because it instantly gives the room a feeling of light. A little variation is added to the white, not with colour, but with glass. As tiles and a bath panel, the glass adds a soft, aqua hue that's really subtle, but enough to lift the look without overwhelming it.

Suite: This chic modern suite is a step up from a traditional white suite. The broad, flat basin has a nicely rounded pedestal and built-in chrome towel rail, invaluable in a small space bathroom like this. To give it a shot of glamour, a glass panel was fixed to the side of the bath – just ask a glazier to cut toughened glass to fit.

Tiles: Walls are covered with large white tiles, creating a backdrop that's less busy-looking than when smaller tiles are used. To tie in with the glass bath panel, glass tiles have been used to line two recessed shelves, adding a subtle hint of blue and waterproofing the surface. The glass-look floor tiles, although expensive, are ultra-modern and very stylish. When floor space is minimal, as here, you can afford to splash out on more expensive flooring.

Storage: Two recessed shelves provide plenty of storage for bathroom bits without eating into the room's space. Before the bath was fitted, a false wall was installed about 10 cm in from the original wall. This conceals pipework and allows space for the recessed shelf to be built.

The look: Nature is the inspiration for this striking bathroom. Rich, lush colours and interesting textures have been teamed beautifully with metal details for a fresh, contemporary look.

Colour: There's a really zingy grass green on the walls in this bathroom, but it's toned down and given a modern edge thanks to the metal of the bath surround and candleholder. The plants add more natural green while the woven chair, storage pot and sisal-effect carpet add more tones from nature and some finger-pleasing texture, too.

Metal: The bath surround and splashback are covered in pre-weathered zinc titanium alloy that won't rust and the candleholder tones in with that. There's more metal woven into the scheme in the form of a galvanized cabinet and a couple of plant pot holders. The mix of shades of grey adds depth and interest to the room, while the chrome taps bring some shine and sparkle.

Plants: If you have a bathroom that gets natural light, plants will grow well in it. The steam from showers and baths suits forest-floor plants like ferns, which will thrive in the slightly damp atmosphere. They also add welcome colour and vibrancy and, in this bathroom, sit neatly on a shelf created by boxing the bath in.

Flooring: This clever carpet looks like natural fibre, but it's actually a lookalike vinyl. Natural flooring doesn't really suit a bathroom, its deep weave acting as a trap for moisture, making it unhygienic. Vinyl is far more practical – and it's also kinder and softer to bare feet.

The look: Light, airy and modern, this small bathroom doesn't have a bath, but instead is fitted with a large walk-in shower. Tiling the walls right up to the ceiling creates a sleek, sparkly finish that helps bounce light around and increases the sense of space.

Shower: A large shower enclosure like this is super-comfortable to use and is streets ahead of the shower over the bath set-up that many bathrooms have. It's safer, too. When climbing in and out of a bath to shower it's easy to slip, and the bath's curved bottom can be precarious. This big shower has none of those problems, but bear in mind before you rip out your bath to install one that many people love to bathe and a house with no bath can put buyers off when you come to sell your property.

Tiling: There's no practical reason to tile right up to the ceiling in a bathroom – it has been done for purely cosmetic reasons. Tiles add a gloss to walls and are tough and hard-wearing. Adding a border around the middle can help a room feel bigger as horizontal stripes give the illusion of space.

Suite: The loo, bidet and basin in this room have the neat proportions and smooth lines of a modern suite. Rounded lines always help make sanitary ware look smaller and more discreet, which is ideal in a compact room like this.

Window: Venetian blinds look crisp and modern hanging at the window and keep out prying eyes while still letting in light. Their orange colour perfectly matches the orange paint of the ceiling.

The look: Modern lighting, glass bricks and plenty of pure white give this bathroom a fresh, cheerful feel. Painting one wall orange peps up the room even more and makes a bold, eye-catching focus.

Colour: Using orange in a bathroom is fun and invigorating, but in a small room like this, it works best on just one wall. If it were painted all over it would make the space feel even smaller. Here, though, it completely changes the feel of this quintessentially modern room. Orange towels add a final shot of zing.

Basin: Basins are typically ceramic, but you can also get them in glass or, as here, chrome. This chrome basin keeps the bathroom looking modern, and its reflective surface bounces light off it. You can find free-standing chrome basins, but this one is inset into a wall unit, that provides extra storage and hides ugly pipe work and the loo cistern.

Splashback: This basin splashback is made of glass as an original alternative to tiling. Ask a glazier to cut some to fit, then just screw it to the wall. It's easy to wipe down and simple to install, too.

Accessories: Accessories are kept to a minimum in this room, to stop the small space feeling cluttered. A rectangular mirror and shelf create strong lines on the wall, and help break up the orange. A few nice-looking bottles are dotted about and because there's nowhere to put a bar of soap on the basin, a chrome liquid-soap dispenser is fixed to the wall.

The look: There's a careful mix of traditional-style bathroom furniture and smart, contemporary accessories in this calm, restful bathroom, giving it stacks of personality and a softly modern feel.

Colour: The theme is blue and white here, but to add interest, a mix of blues has been used. A sky-blue on the lower half of the walls and in the curtain mixes with a fresher turquoise under the bath and a paler blue high up the walls. Floor tiles in two similar blues complete the look, and the white suite and plenty of white woodwork stop the room from looking overwhelmingly colourful.

Suite: A reproduction roll-top bath begs you to lie back for a long soak, and its position by the window means you can peep outside at the stars while you do. A traditional-style basin with generous proportions and strong lines adds further old-school luxury, its chunky shape perfectly suited to a spacious room like this.

Splashback: Toughened glass makes an excellent splashback because it's sleek, discreet, allows you to see the wall colour through it and can be cut to fit any size. Here, it accentuates the aqua colour of the walls – a really nice effect.

Accessories: Although the suite is traditional, the chrome shelving unit and big round mirror bring the room up to date. Open storage space for towels and bottles looks great and keeps the space uncluttered, which is essential for an airy, calm feel.

The look: From the oversized white tiles to the shell-encrusted mirror and huge sparkly ball hanging from the ceiling, this bright, white bathroom is unique and undeniably creative.

Colour: White is the theme here, with a white suite and white tiles covering the walls. They give the room shine and brightness and make it feel as big as possible. To break it up a little, skirting boards are painted soft green and there are rich red towels on the shiny chrome rack. The shells on the ornate mirror also have soft, delicate colour in them.

Suite: This modern suite has generous proportions and smooth lines. The basin has a built-in towel rail and a wide, deep bowl. The taps add a fun note. In shiny chrome with blue knobs and details, they look modern, but also quirky – just right for this bathroom.

Mirror: A piece of mirror glass was cut into this curvy shape by a glazier, then stuck to a larger MDF base. Shells and mosaic were then stuck onto the MDF using PVA adhesive to create this texture-rich design. The best way to dust an intricate frame like this is with a soft paintbrush, to shift dust gently without risking dislodging any shells.

Flooring: Ceramic tiles have been laid on this floor to create a watertight base. Rather than line the floor tiles up with those on the wall, they have been laid at an angle to give the room more movement and stop it feeling too boxy or geometric.

The look: This bathroom shouts grown-up sophistication, with its lavish, curvy suite, smart black and blue tiles and luxurious walk-in shower.

Colour: A smart-as-you-like colour scheme of black, turquoise and white gives this bathroom plenty of sleek style. Turquoise painted walls match large turquoise wall tiles, broken up by a band of black mosaic. A white suite and floor tiles look fresh and clean, while flashes of chrome give the room shine and contemporary style.

Suite: This suite takes the generous proportions and curved shapes of old-style bathrooms and gives them a modern flavour. The large basin has a traditional looking pedestal, but its big bowl has the soft lines of modern design. Round chrome taps look up-to-date, but pleasingly soft and stylish, while the chrome shower with its simple white shower tray is modern but unpretentious.

Walls: The mixture of large wall tiles and smaller mosaics gives the walls far more interest than if tiles of all one size were used. The black border breaks up the blue above and below, and also accentuates the room's size – horizontal lines always make a room feel bigger. Black mosaic also gives the room a strong, sexy, slightly masculine feel.

Floor: White ceramic floor tiles make for a fresh, hygienic surface. They bounce light upwards, helping the room feel brighter and give the suite the impression of melting into them, which in turn helps the room feel spacious and seamless. Floor tiles are a very hygienic choice in a bathroom, but they can feel cold underfoot. Think carefully before fitting them and consider underfloor heating – the height of luxury.

The look: It's not so much the shape of the suite (which is very traditional) or the layout of this bathroom that makes it feel modern, but the use of colour. A light, zingy turquoise and a rich purple have been used to inject some brightness into this dark room, giving it knock-out contemporary style.

Colour: A rich purple has been used on the wooden panelling that runs around the lower half of this bathroom, giving the room warmth, drama and depth. To stop it feeling small or dark, a brighter shade – a fresh turquoise – has been used on the walls above lightening the look and giving the room lots of energy. A mountain of towels in variations on these two shades add a dash more colour, as do plants in pink pots on the windowsill.

Walls: Bright turquoise is not the only thing to adorn these walls. To help the room feel bigger and lighter, four wavy mirrors have been hung side by side. They look more interesting and stylish than a plain, rectangular mirror, adding a wave-like motif to a room that is, after all, about water. Panelling on the lower part of the walls creates a cosy, cottagey feel that's given a very modern twist thanks to a splash of purple paint.

Accessories: This room is brimming with interesting accessories that look good and work hard, earning their place in the small space. A curvy shelving unit provides room for towels and essentials, and it ties in nicely with the shiny chrome of the taps, soap dish and tooth mug holder. An elegant candle sconce on the wall is also in metal. It looks gorgeous and provides a safe place for lit candles in this compact room.

CONTEMPORARY

The look: It's fresh, colourful and clean – a bathroom to put you in a great mood. Coloured tiles, cheery wallpaper and a contemporary white suite combine to make a room that is both stylish and practical.

Colour: Bright blues, turquoises and green feature in this modern bathroom, giving it heaps of energy, while lashings of white add necessary freshness and brighten the colour. Accessories are in similar shades of blue to create a relaxed, coordinated look.

Suite: Smooth, curvy lines and minimal details are the stylish hallmarks of a contemporary suite. The loo has a simply styled narrow cistern while the basin has a lovely rounded bowl and fuss-free pedestal. It all helps the room feel light and easy to live with.

Tiling: Both floor and walls are tiled in this bathroom. The sparkly white floor is given a lift at low level by large coloured tiles on the walls, which draw the eye to the lower part of the room. White tiles above create a feeling of height, then the vertical lines of the stripy wallpaper carry your gaze to the ceiling. It's a clever technique that makes the room feel bigger. For variety, there's a 'crazy paved' basin splashback, made of pieces of navy tiles stuck in a random pattern. This contrasts with the squareness of the tiles on wall and floor.

Accessories: Accessories are kept to a minimum so the fresh, open feel of this bathroom isn't spoilt. Towels, a photo frame, even the soap are all in matching blues while touches of shiny chrome on the towel rail and cup holder are just right in this sparkly room.

The look: There's an Eastern flavour to this stylish bathroom. Dark wood, clean lines and sculptural flowers in the window give it a refined, calming, sophisticated feel, fresh from the Orient.

Colour: Colour is soft and muted here to create a very relaxed but sophisticated atmosphere. Off-white walls and oatmeal-coloured floor and wall tiles are given serious sex appeal by the dark wooden bath surround, picture frames and the small table.

Suite: This suite is minimal, modern and unfussy without looking austere. Its soft lines give it a relaxed feel, and neat, rounded taps keep the lines flowing smoothly. The bath's smart dark wooden surround makes a bold statement in the room. Although it stands out, it's perfectly in keeping with the room's mood of Zen-like calm. It's streamlined and very tasteful.

Floor: Ceramic floor tiles are the perfect watertight and tough surface for a bathroom. Here, large tiles have been used, ideal in this spacious room, although they could look out of proportion in a smaller room. Their oatmeal colour makes them subtle and discreet, a neutral backdrop for the attractive suite.

Accessories: These are kept to a minimum so the space feels uncluttered and calm, but that's not to say it's devoid of detail. Good quality bath products are arranged on a dark wood table at the end of the bath – a stylish way to keep them on hand, if you have space. Another eye-catching ingredient is the bamboo towel ladder. This perfectly captures the Eastern theme, and provides invaluable extra storage, too.

The look: This room is sunny, elegant and charmingly old-world in style. The suite is reminiscent of a country house from the 1920s, while the colours, flooring and accessories are brimming with understated elegance.

Colour: White dominates this room, making it feel spacious, airy and clean. Both the walls and the suite are white, but touches of subtle colour break it up. There are dark notes – the picture frames, loo seat, bath feet – and soft notes – the pale blue on the underside of the bath and in the flooring. They don't detract from the white scheme, but do help give it warmth and depth.

Suite: This suite is a reproduction of a bathroom from the 1920s or 1930s. The roll-top bath, high-level WC with overhead cistern and strong, shapely lines are complemented by traditional chrome-plated taps and mixers.

The underside of the bath is painted a soft blue to accentuate its shape, while taps and a hand-held shower are mounted in the centre so either end is comfortable for lying back against.

Walls: Panelled walls give any room a strong, traditional feel. They can be fitted in any room (though can make small rooms feel more enclosed) and create an elegant, country house feel. Painted white, they look simple and stylish, adding interest to the walls without the need of colour.

Accessories: These have been carefully chosen to continue the traditional feel. The loo roll holder, towel rail and shelf all have the same strong lines and old-style feel as the suite, while framed old photos add interest and keep the bathroom rooted in the past. Cosmetics and toiletries are hidden away, so nothing modern jars with the room's traditional feel.

The look: There is a mix of influences at work in this bathroom. Set against the cool lilac and white scheme is a Venetian mirror, a Moroccan lantern and a cupboard with a Swedish feel. They work harmoniously together to create a look that's both stylish and individual.

Colour: The softest lilac has been used on the walls, creating a peaceful ambience. It's teamed with an even paler greyish lilac on the wooden panelling, which sits next to the soft white of the tiled floor. A white suite adds freshness, while towels, soap and even the hyacinths on the cabinet match the lilac and white theme.

Suite: This white suite has a few shapely details that give it a soft, feminine edge, perfect for this soothing, pretty room. The cistern and basin-back are gently arched while the basin bowl has a grooved rim, showing off its rounded line.

Window: Instead of curtains, the glass in this window has been covered with self-adhesive opaque film with a criss-cross pattern. It looks incredibly stylish, keeps out prying eyes, but still lets light in. It also looks far neater than a blind or curtains and its criss-cross pattern is picked up in the lantern.

Accessories: There are some stunning pieces in this room. The show-stopping mirror is Venetian, an elegant classic, while the lantern has a North African flavour. The little table, with its white finish and neat lines, fits in perfectly and provides space for storing towels. A cabinet tucked into an alcove has storage for everyday bathroom bits and its gingham inset door picks up the room's colour scheme.

The look: A window at one end fills this oblong bathroom with natural light, which is boosted by and bounced off miles of sparkling white tiles and two long mirrors, set high on opposite walls. Original 1930s tiles inspired an Art Deco look, with chequer-board flooring and a chunky, old-style suite.

Colour: The suite, walls and ceiling are mostly white, creating a bright, open feel. Dashes of colour crop up on the walls where two fine borders of original 1930s tiles in rich green break up the white tiles. On the floor, blue and white chequer-board tiles add more deep colour to anchor the room and are in keeping with the 1930s look.

Mirrors: Mirrors don't have to be just for looking into. This bathroom shows how two long mirrors can really brighten up a room. Set high up on the walls – too high to see comfortably into them – they instead earn their keep by reflecting light around the room and increasing the illusion of space – useful, in what is quite a narrow room.

Suite: The strong, solid lines and big dimensions of this suite date it firmly in the 1930s (even though it's repro!). Two built-in towel rails on either side of the basin are authentic details and also incredibly useful, while the bath's wooden panelling has a boxy, Art Deco-flavoured design. The panelling has also been cleverly designed with a small cupboard at the end – ideal for storing bathroom essentials like loo roll out of sight.

Floor: Chequer-board designs are very 1930s in feel and add a little drama and life to a floor. In a long room like this, they also have the effect of leading the eye up the room, helping to make it feel larger.

The look: Natural wood, fluffy towels and soft, pale shades give this bathroom a cool, stylish feel. Here, slate flooring has been used to great effect, creating a dark, textured backdrop for the white suite.

Colour: This bathroom teams a white suite and white woodwork with soft blue walls and lots of pale watery-blue towels. Natural wood in glowing honey tones adds warm notes to the scheme, and rich, dark, textured slate tiles create a rough and sexy natural flooring that looks dramatic against the sleek white bath.

Accessories: There's plenty of wood in this room, giving it a natural, organic feel. A wooden slatted bath mat makes a nice alternative to traditional towelling mats, and a set of scales with a wooden surround tones in well. A wooden bath rack provides plenty of storage space for a back brush, loofah, bath oils and soap. The bentwood Shaker-style laundry bin also works as a useful side table to the basin.

Suite: This reproduction roll-top bath is made from acrylic so it's lighter and warmer than a traditional cast-iron design. It has claw feet, just as an original model would, but they're made from modern, shiny chrome. The basin has a fittingly old-world look, with a sculpted pedestal, shapely basin bowl and chunky taps.

Flooring: Slate is hardwearing, handsome and water resistant, so it's great in a bathroom. These tiles are unpolished so they create a slightly uneven surface that's tactile and rustic.

The look: This bathroom mixes old and new with confidence. A period-feel suite sits happily alongside the antique cast-iron fireplace, while fresh white tiles get a shot of modern glamour thanks to a thin silver border. Instead of conventional frosted glass, this window has coloured and frosted panes that are both stylish and practical.

Colour: The walls are painted in a soft, warm grey to provide a gentle backdrop for the dramatic window and dark slate floor. The blue glass of the window panes is complemented by a row of blue glass vases on the mantelpiece and the blue glass in the mirror's frame. The white tiles and suite add freshness.

Window: A lively, chequer-board effect gives this sash window oodles of style. Blue stained glass and matt, opaque-effect panes stop the world looking in, but still let lots of light pour through. On sunny days, the coloured panes create a pretty pattern of blue light across the floor and wall.

Floor: These slate tiles in grey-black work beautifully with the black fireplace. The 30 cm x 30 cm tiles were cut in half to make a border around the walls to replace the skirting board. Slate tiles are ideal for a bathroom because they're waterproof, easy to clean and hard wearing, but you may find them a little cold underfoot. If you'd prefer something warmer, try vinyl flooring instead – kinder to toes, but just as practical.

Tiles: Plain white tiles are a can't fail addition to any bathroom, guaranteed never to go out of fashion, but if you think they're a little boring, opt for tiles with a textured finish like these. A matt silver profile strip peps up the look yet more, helping to break up the tall wall of tiles and frame the stepped pattern.

The look: This vibrant bathroom combines a mix of bright blue mosaics, blue and white tiles and dark granite flooring to create a colourful, eclectic look. Light pours in both from the window and through glass tiles, inset in the far wall.

Suite: Roll-top baths are very popular today and because they're free-standing rather than boxed off and enclosed, they can make a bathroom feel bigger, as you can see the floor stretching away beneath them. It's possible to buy restored original cast-iron baths, but they can be expensive. A cheaper alternative is to pick up a new, acrylic bath in a traditional style. Here, brass taps add to the traditional feel and are mounted in the centre of the bath so you can laze in comfort at either end.

Floor: Reclaimed granite tiles from a salvage yard take up most of this floor, but because there weren't enough to cover it completely, blue and white tiles have been added around the basin pedestal and below the tub to finish off. These tie in nicely with the blue mosaic and give the floor an individual, stylish feel.

Walls: Mosaic tiles create a waterproof barrier around the bath and a single line of them has been continued up along the wall borders and ceiling to frame the room. Three rows of glass bricks, fitted into the wall, allow more light to flood in and create an attractive feature, set off by the candle sconces between them. A background of plain white lets the blue tiles sing out and continues the fresh feel.

The look: This bathroom has an eye-catching, Indian theme – vibrant pinks and purples are teamed with dark wooden furniture and a scattering of exotic accessories.

Colour: To carry off a strong look like this, you need to mix colours carefully. Too many hot shades and the room will feel overbearing and claustrophobic, too few and the Indian theme will be lost. Here, a soothing lilac on the walls creates a subtly colourful backdrop, letting the shocking pink bath tub and dark wooden furniture stand out. White paintwork adds freshness.

Bath: A characterful bath, like this old roll-top one with brass taps, works brilliantly with the Indian look. In addition, its underside has been painted a bright-as-you-like pink, then a paisley pattern was stencilled onto it in brown paint to create a henna-tattoo look.

Furniture: Chunky, dark wooden furniture captures the Indian look perfectly. As a stylish alternative to blinds or curtains, invest in a gorgeous carved wooden screen. It will keep out prying eyes while letting sunlight peep through and throw beautiful shadows on the floor. A decorative look like this relies on pretty pieces that aren't included just for practical reasons, so there's a tiny, carved wooden shelf, painted in a darker purple on the wall with flowers and artwork perched on it.

Floor: When you have lots of colour in a room and plenty of accessories to draw your eye, it's a good idea to keep the floor neutral, so it doesn't compete for attention. These pale ceramic tiles are perfect.

The look: There's a relaxed, worn-about-the-edges look to this vast bathroom, where individual pieces rather than a coordinated suite take pride of place. An old peeling tub, rusting enamel vase and distressed chest give this room stacks of character, with each piece given plenty of space to breathe thanks to the room's generous dimensions.

Colour: Faded colours suit the faded elegance of the furniture in this room. Cool cream on the walls and off-white on the floorboards provide the perfect backdrop. A moth-eaten cushion with a frayed red and cream cover adds a dash of colour, but in a really relaxed low-key way.

Bath: The bath is a French bateau bath, incredibly deep and heavy. If you're lucky, you can find pieces like this at salvage yards, or hop across the channel and look in France. The taps are not as old as the bath, but have an equally aged appearance. They're mounted on the wall, leaving both ends of the tub free for wallowing.

Window: Even the blind is reclaimed in this house. It comes from New England and dates from the 19th century. It's totally in keeping with the peeling, but appealing, look of this room.

Furniture: There's lots of space to continue the lived in look here. An old wooden stool makes a decorative addition to one corner, with a rusting pitcher, flowers and candlesticks on top. An old school locker, stripped back to its original paint, provides storage under the window, while a 1930s rag-rug softens the bare boards. Again, have a nose around fleamarkets or salvage yards for similar gems.

The look: There's a fresh, seaside feel to this bathroom. A colour scheme of rich blues reminds you of sea and sky, while the panelled walls are straight out of a beach hut or windswept shore-line cottage.

Colour: Deep blue is warm and dramatic but, as with all dark shades, can make a room feel smaller. To stop that happening here it has only been painted on the woodwork that runs around the lower part of the room and up one wall. Above, a softer blue keeps the look light and airy, while the white suite adds yet more freshness.

Walls: The wood panelling not only gives the room a slightly rustic edge, it's also been used to cover old tile work. It's an easy way to hide tiles and saves the effort of chipping them off, replastering and retiling. A shiny chrome toothbrush and loo roll holder have been firmly fixed to the panelling, by screwing into the supporting battens behind.

Window: To cover some less than stylish patterned panes, glass shelves have been fitted by a glazier in front of the window, then empty blue water bottles and glass night light holders have been lined up on them. They hide the glass, but allow the light to flood in, plus you can have a candlelit bath whenever you feel like it.

Accessories: A mahogany style loo seat and a dark wood cabinet complement the suite's traditional feel and add some deep, warm colour to the room. Towels and bath mat, meanwhile, are in matching shades of blue to keep the room coordinated.

The look: Ditsy florals and pretty pastel shades give this bathroom a feminine, country-cottage feel that is forever England. A stylish basin set into a wall unit and smart tiled floor bring the room up to date without spoiling the charming cottagey feel.

Colour: A country scheme cries out for warm, pastel shades. Here, soft creams, muted pinks and the palest mint green all sit happily side by side. It doesn't matter how many shades you mix into a room like this, just make sure they're all the same strength, or one will leap out and dominate the others.

Suite: This modern basin has lovely smooth lines – sharp edges don't suit a country-look bathroom. Set in a built-in unit, it looks discreet and pretty. The wooden worktop adds to the rustic feel while the traditional shape of the gleaming chrome taps adds old-style appeal and stops the basin looking too contemporary.

Floor: Ceramic floor tiles are a hard-working, practical choice for a bathroom. To suit the soft look of this room, these tiles are in a warm, toffee shade that fits right in with all those faded pastels. The wooden bath mat adds a touch of wholesome country authenticity.

Walls: Floral-patterned wallpaper is an absolutely classic country look. A soft, repeat rose design is subtle and won't dominate the room. To protect the paper behind the basin, a sheet of toughened glass is fixed to the wall. This allows the pattern still to be seen, but prevents splashes from damaging it.

The look: Inspired by the generous feel of a 1930s hotel bathroom, this one has a bath with luxurious, out-sized proportions, an angular basin and chunky chrome taps. A fresh blue colour scheme brings the room bang up-to-date and there's a modern shower over the bath, too.

Suite: The strong lines and generous proportions of this bathroom suite give it a real 1930s feel. Wall-mounted taps are more expensive to fit, but make filling a bath like this one, that's tucked into a recess, easier – no stretching round to turn them on. Shiny chrome taps and plugs complete the modern country look.

Towel ladder: In a small room with limited wall space, it can be tricky to fit a radiator in. Instead, take advantage of the room's height by fitting a vertical, ladder-style towel radiator. This one has a retro style to help it fit in with the 1930s-look suite.

Walls: The walls are clad with special waterproof MDF panels, made to look like tongue and groove boarding, with a plate rack trim about three quarters of the way up. Above is plasterwork, painted a slightly paler shade of blue than the panelling.

Accessories: A round mirror looks simple and elegant mounted on the panelled walls. Choose one that can pivot on hinges like this, to give greater flexibility. A matching glass and chrome shelf provides storage for toothbrushes and soap, while towels in shades of blue and turquoise tone in with the colour of the walls.

The look: Salvaged Victorian tiles are the basis for the colour scheme in this welcoming, country-style bathroom. Cladding the walls and sides of the bath with reeded panelling painted a creamy white, enhances the country feel, and little splashes of mushroom, lilac and blue add subtle interest.

Floor: Using salvage-yard finds like these patterned tiles is a sure-fire way to inject oceans of character into your room. Here, there were only enough to tile a square in the centre of the room, but it was easy to find toning fawn tiles to complete the floor.

Colour: Cream is a classic country shade – softer and less chilly than pure white, but just as easy to coordinate with other colours. Here, mushroom is the colour used most with cream, but bleached out rather than strong blues are also dotted around, for a faded, lived-in, country air.

Window: To increase the laid-back country feel, the Roman blind is made from incredibly fine linen in two colours – blue and soft brown. It's left down to hide an ugly view over a bleak brick wall, providing privacy without blocking out light.

Accessories: All the bits and bobs in this room add to its restful, homely style. The untreated wooden frames on a couple of inexpensive mirrors were painted soft colours and a nifty flannel rack has been knocked up from a length of wood that's been painted then had clothes pegs nailed in place. Just add a retro-style bath rack, *et voilà* – the room is complete.

The look: There's a fresh, country feel to this bathroom, but thanks to some clever modern tricks and a shapely suite, it has a contemporary twist, too.

Colour: A mix of spring-like greens gives this bathroom a sunny freshness. The panelled walls are painted a pale yellowy green while the bath surround, basin wall and skirting have a deeper mossier green. The suite is in a soft off-white, perfect for a country-style scheme – bright white could look too harsh and modern.

Suite: This suite's smooth lines and swanky mixer taps shout contemporary design. The unusual wall-mounted basin is eye-catching, midway between a traditional pedestal basin and a modern bowl-style one, but while the shapes are up to date, they're versatile, too – soft enough to suit any scheme. Rather than just mounting the basin on the wall, a low wall has been built at the end of the bath so it can face inwards – again, a modern touch that gives this bathroom extra style points.

Walls: The walls have been panelled with wood to create a cosy, country feel. Unlike traditional tongue-and-groove, which has deep grooves, this panelling is sleek and streamlined – a modern take on the rustic look. A generous wooden border around the window frames it beautifully. It's an unusual touch and looks great, tying in with the wooden bath surround and deep moulded skirting.

Shelves: These hang from the ceiling, rather than being wall-mounted. This means you can reach their contents from the basin or the bath – a practical touch – and the walls' neat panelling isn't disturbed. Plus, of course, they look fantastic. The creamy wood has a touch of country style, but the way they're hung is very modern.

The look: Comfy, cosy and ever so slightly ramshackle, this unassuming bathroom is country style at its most simple. The room is light, functional and welcoming, with easy, laid-back style.

Colour: Cream, cream and more cream. It's a country-style classic, and warms up this bathroom while still keeping it light and airy. A white suite adds a shot of snowy brightness, but its freshness is softened by the cream walls and floor.

Walls: The walls are part panelled, which divides them in half and gives them a rustic feel. Both the panelling and plasterwork are painted with the same cream, but it's a good idea to use an oil-based paint on wooden panelling to protect it from splashes.

Suite: A plain white suite is given a country feel with brass, rather than chrome, taps and handles. Chrome taps are unmistakably modern, but golden, copper or brass-coloured ones give a bathroom a slightly 19th-century feel. They also tone in beautifully with the creamy scheme.

Accessories: Cut flowers in a bathroom are a real treat, and instantly give a simple room an air of luxury and romance. Here, cream roses are displayed in a pretty Shaker-style basket, hanging from the wall. A single picture is the only other adornment, so the room stays uncluttered and restful.

COUNTRY

The look: There's a sea theme in this bathroom, with a bluey-green on the walls and the same colour, mixed with varnish, painted onto the floor. The rough finish on the floorboards, wire-fronted cupboards and buckets used as storage give the room a rustic, beach house feel.

Colour: Bluey-green is a popular colour for a bathroom, because it has a water-like tone and creates a cool, calm feel. White tiles and suite are the ideal accompaniment to this classic bathroom colourway.

Floor: To give the boards some colour, a mix of emulsion and varnish was painted on. Numerous feet walking over it has left the finish distressed – a weatherbeaten look that's straight out of a seaside cottage.

Cupboard: A built-in cupboard in a bathroom is a real asset, providing lots of space for storing towels and bath products. Here, the wooden panels in the doors have been replaced with wire mesh, allowing you to see inside and giving the cupboard informal, country style.

Accessories: With its big cupboard and generous dimensions there's plenty of space for accessories in this room. An old rocking horse from a boot fair and a sweet, personalized life ring are the room's most eye-catching ingredients, giving it stacks of rustic character. An enormous mirror helps the room feel bigger still, while old buckets and galvanized wall-mounted storage provide a home for bathroom bits.

The look: This short-on-space bathroom gets a vibrant shot of colour thanks to glowing, bright yellow walls. A white suite, fun artwork and whitewashed tongue-and-groove panelling cool the vibrancy for a look that's invigorating and sunny.

Colour: There's nothing timid about the yellow on these walls – it's pure sunshine. While a strong shade like this would give you a headache used in a large room, in this tiny bathroom there's just enough of it to add brightness and energy, without it dominating. The whitewashed panelling and white suite help cool the yellow and balance it, while the large painting breaks it up still further, adding some further colours, too. Navy towels tie in with the blue of the painting and contrast dramatically with the yellow.

Wood panelling: You can't beat wood panelling for instantly giving a bathroom a slightly rustic, countrified feel. Here, it's the perfect laid-back balance to all that vigorous, modern yellow. The whitewashed effect was created by mixing white emulsion with water then brushing over. To protect the wood from splashes, a couple of coats of clear varnish have been painted on top.

Storage: The back of the door is a prime storage location for towels, invaluable in a small bathroom. Here, two big shiny hooks make a home for them. An old wine bottle box, fixed to the wall, makes more informal storage – a place for towels or bottles – and adds to the room's rustic feel. Look for old wooden crates like this at flea markets or salvage yards – they cost just a few pounds.

The look: Colour is king in this zingy green bathroom. A plain white suite creates a fresh contrast against the bright lime walls while a dark wooden floor adds a welcome note of sobriety to the vibrant scene.

Colour: Green and white is the theme here, with a dark, lime-green shade painted onto the tongue-and-groove walls, and a softer, fresher green painted above it. A border of white between the two creates definition and ties in with the white suite. Green accessories (the bin, the face cloths) and an old white-painted chair are the finishing touches.

Suite: If you live in a Victorian or Edwardian house, you might like to buy a traditional-style suite that's in keeping with your home's age. Traditional-style basins don't need to look big and heavy. This neat design has a pretty, tapering pedestal and is less bulky than some on the market. The reproduction roll-top bath has bags of retro style, but it's actually double-skinned acrylic, rather than cast-iron, so it retains the water heat longer and weighs less.

Floor: Wooden floors make a good, hygienic base for a bathroom and these dark boards add warmth to the room, too. Just make sure they are coated with a suitably waterproof varnish, to protect them from the inevitable splashes and drips.

Walls: Tongue-and-groove instantly adds a country feel to any bathroom. It's also a useful way to cover pipework or uneven plasterwork. Unless you're a confident DIYer, get a carpenter to fit it and paint with an oil-based paint to protect the wood from moisture.

The look: This is a light, bright bathroom with a simple blue and white scheme that makes the most of the natural light flooding through the tall window. Comfort is key here, so a blue carpet provides a soft surface for bare feet and is comfortable enough for babies and kids to roll about on after bathtime.

Colour: This is an easy colour scheme to pull off – just stick to white predominantly then add the odd splash of blue to rev it up. There are no rules about colour in a bathroom, but blue, green and aqua shades are a natural choice in a room that's all about water.

Suite: This white suite has a few stylish twists that give it more character than the average suite. The bath surround is sculpted and shaped and the loo's pedestal has a matching lined design. Most striking of all is the blue loo seat – fun, colourful and a hit with kids.

Tiles: All-white tiles could have left this bathroom looking bleached out. Instead, beautiful hand-painted tiles with a textured surface are mixed in with standard white tiles. This not only looks effective, it's also a great-value way to make a few expensive coloured tiles go further.

Window: If you have a big window in your bathroom that's well away from the suite and won't get splashed, you can afford to hang a curtain at it. This white tab-top curtain can be left drawn during the day without depriving the room of light because it's made from fine, filmy material that filters the sunlight and suits the room's fresh, breezy feel.

The look: Leaping dolphin tiles, a shell encrusted loo seat and mirror, and plenty of sand-coloured tiles give this room a fun feel, inspired by the seaside.

Colour: The walls are painted magnolia to create a neutral backdrop that tones in with the cream mosaic tiles running around the room. Sand-coloured towels add to the neutral scheme, and pretty shells with brown and cream patterns dotted about create lots of eye-catching detail. A border of tiles with a black dolphin design is the *pièce-de-resistance*, injecting heaps of fun into the room, and a splash of darker colour, too.

Tiles: Mosaic tiles are fitted half way up the walls in this bathroom. Although that's a lot of tiling, their soft, creamy colour means they don't dominate the room. They are given energy and drama with a border of rectangular tiles with a dolphin design. This divides the creamy tiles from the magnolia walls – a combination that could look a little boring otherwise – and the horizontal band helps make the room feel bigger.

Suite: This plain white suite has shiny chrome taps and handles and a soft, tapered edge, adding to the gentle, welcoming feel of the room. No opportunity to continue the seaside theme has been lost here, so, to jazz up the loo a little, there's a seat embedded with shells that looks fun and witty – a guaranteed hit with children, too.

Accessories: A matching towel rail and loo roll holder have a distinctive shell design. More shells appear embedded in the mirror's frame, and a selection are scattered on top of the loo cistern and on the shelf that boxes off the pipework, so there's plenty to touch and enjoy here.

The look: A soothing dusky pink colour scheme and neat, elegant bathroom suite give this room bags of understated style. Storage boxes on the walls look great, are incredibly practical and mean there's lots for youngsters to look at and enjoy.

Colour: The soft colours were inspired by a selection of sea shells. Dusky pink on the walls looks subtle without making the room feel small, as a stronger pink would. A creamy suite tones in perfectly, without the jarring effect of white, while stone-coloured floor and wall tiles add more warm, neutral tones and keep the atmosphere calm.

Suite: This smart, stylish suite was actually a budget buy from one of the large DIY stores, proving that it's not necessary to spend a lot to get bathroom furniture that's well designed. The loo cistern is tall and slim, so it takes up little wall space, while the basin has smooth lines and a compact shape.

Radiator: This clever design combines a radiator and towel warmer in one. An old-style radiator forms the centre with shiny chrome pipework around it providing space for drying towels. It's compact, too, fitting neatly into this spatially challenged room.

Storage: By boxing in the bath, extra storage has been created. There's a tiled shelf at one end where rattan boxes are stacked while underneath a cupboard is hidden, accessed via a door, where bathroom essentials like loo rolls and harmful substances like bleach can be stored safely away from children.

The look: The simplicity of this bathroom makes it ideal for both adults and kids. Pretty, friendly colours, a big tub with simple taps, and bathroom bits stored out of the way of young hands, mean children will love this room, while adults will enjoy the soothing colours and clean lines – perfect for after-work relaxing.

Colour: Lavender is a very restful shade and looks clean and simple teamed with white. Stripy tiles blend the white and lavender theme perfectly and create an interesting splashback to the bath, while touches of warm natural wood (the picture frames and shelf), add just the right amount of tonal variety.

Suite: This suite is all about simple modern styling at its best. Lines are soft and flowing (just right for a room that children will use), and the basin has generous proportions without looking intrusive.

There's no shower attachment here. This is a simple room – bathing in a big tub with elegant, discreet taps is what it's all about.

Floor: White wooden floorboards are both colour-coordinated and practical. Painted and sealed they are perfectly water resistant, which is essential, as kids plus baths equals lots of splashes. A soft lavender mat adds a further coordinated note, warming up a big expanse of white and providing a soft landing when you step out of the bath.

Accessories: Cluttered bathrooms and kids don't mix, so this room has plenty of shelving (as the reflection in the mirror shows), to store all the bathroom essentials, so the rest of the space is clear. A pretty, etched mirror brings a contemporary note to the room, but elsewhere pieces are simple and timeless.

The look: This light, stylish bathroom will appeal to adults and children alike. It's warm and inviting with enough interest and detail to mean there's something for everyone to pick up, look at and enjoy.

Colour: The suite is classically shaped and plain white so it is easy to team colour with. A mix of soft green walls and beige tiles go together, with a matching beige blind that has a subtle feather and pebble pattern on it. Further shades of beige, soft brown and jade are introduced with storage baskets, towels and flooring. A wooden cabinet provides one contrasting note of darker, more dramatic colour.

Walls: The tiling on the walls is taken up quite high, primarily to protect the wall around the bath from splashes from both boisterous kids and the hand-held shower attachment. The tiling also neatly covers the boxed-off pipework at the end of the bath and below the sink. Covering this much of the walls in plain beige tiles could look a little drab, so to create some interest, textured tiles have been chosen, their uneven surfaces beautifully catching and reflecting the light.

Storage: Great use has been made of the many different surfaces in this bathroom. Shelves created through boxing-off the pipework, space at the end of the bath and the windowsill have been transformed into storage with jars, baskets and beakers. A wooden cabinet on the wall keeps more bathroom bits out of reach or children's hands, but its slatted front means you can easily see what's inside. A large sisal basket makes space for laundry or towels and its beige colour fits right in with the room's scheme.

The look: This bright, airy bathroom has plenty of colour and interest in it to please the eye and amuse children. Turquoise walls, lilac and black tiles and a handsome wooden floor make it welcoming and energizing, plus there's plenty of shelving and surface space for keeping essentials close to hand.

Colour: There are three key colours in this room: turquoise, lilac and black. Old swirly wallpaper has been quickly covered up with a lick of zingy turquoise paint teamed with a softer shade of lilac on the woodwork, bath panelling and even across some tiles. A border of black tiles around the window and the bath area adds definition.

Tiling: Predominantly white tiles line the bath area to a good height, so it's safe to have a shower in here, too, and kids splashing won't harm the walls. To break the white up, thin, rectangular tiles have been used to create a border around the tiling and in lines across the middle of the white area. Some are black, but others have been painted lilac to match the woodwork. Painting tiles is a great way to give them a new lease of life. Pop to your local DIY store and check out the specialist tile paint on sale. A basin splashback of tiles with a shell motif on them is the final detail and looks pretty and fun.

Panelling: Tongue-and-groove panelling has been used to encase the bath and box-off pipework below the basin. Painted lilac, it looks fun and countrified and keeps the look informal and family-friendly. Boxing off pipes has also created a useful shelf for bathroom bits.

The look: Simple, colourful and with plenty of clean, uncluttered space, this is the perfect family bathroom. Half-tiled walls ensure the area around the bath and basin is splash-resistant, while a high shelf stores bathroom bottles out of reach of young hands.

Colour: Green and yellow are a springtime combination that perfectly suits this sunny room. White glossed woodwork and a gleaming white suite add plenty of complementary freshness, while a pale wooden floor helps the room feel even bigger and brighter.

Suite: This simple modern suite has easy-to-live-with soft lines and rounded rims. The bath has been fitted in a window recess, helping to make the room feel even more spacious and uncluttered. A hand-held shower attachment is a useful addition in a bathroom that children use. You can use it to hose them down or wash hair, with far more control than with a conventional shower. You can also use it to rinse the bath after grubby kids have splashed it.

Window: Fitting the bath in the window recess means the windowsill acts as a useful shelf for bathroom bits. As a result, there's less need for bulky cabinets or storage that would make the room feel cluttered. A simple roller blind can be drawn down to any length, depending on what's on the sill, while a couple of coats of gloss ensure the sill is watertight.

Accessories: Accessories are kept to a minimum here, to ensure the room feels airy and serene. Two skinny rails have been placed above the bath taps so towels are on hand before you've even stepped out of the bath. A glass shelf above looks sleek and discreet and keeps bathroom bottles out of kids' reach. Flowers add a further spring-like touch to the room, while a toothbrush holder and soap dish that match the suite look neatly coordinated.

The look: Easy, welcoming style is what this bathroom is all about. There's room for a free-standing shower and a big, double-ended bath, and there's plenty of storage for everybody's bathing bits. The room has soft carpet, soft colours and soft lines – a style that will suit adults and children alike.

Suite: A double-ended bath is ideal if you have two children – they can both bathe comfortably at the same time, saving hot water and energy. This one has generous proportions and smooth lines. The matching basin has the same soft lines, while the shower is a little more traditional. A huge rose allows plenty of water to flood out and mosaic tiles keep the whole space watertight.

Colour: Soft pink and off-white are the background shades for this room. They're subtle and easy to live with, but not as cold as pure white can be. A green shower curtain and a raspberry bath mat liven up the scheme.

Storage: If you have the space and you like to have your toiletries to hand, putting up a long shelf can solve your storage problems in one. This shelf is dotted with pretty bottles, vases and candles – practical and good looking.

Floor: Tiles are the most practical choice for a bathroom floor, but carpet makes a soft floor covering that's particularly welcome in a room where you're often barefoot. Check with the manufacturer first that it is moisture resistant and suitable for a bathroom.

The look: Thanks to a huge window, there's plenty of natural light in this spacious bathroom, and the soft blue and fresh white colour scheme really makes the most of it. There's an old-style feel to the suite and accessories, while a smattering of shells, a cute mat and a pebble or two add some seaside flavour and provide lots for both adults and children to look at and enjoy.

Colour: To give the walls an open-sky feel, they've been painted with a blue wash that looks lighter and softer than a solid finish. To do this, first paint walls white then brush on a watered-down mix of emulsion using broad, irregular strokes, so the white peeps through.

Suite: A reproduction roll-top bath with claw feet teams brilliantly with the basin and loo thanks to their chunky, retro shape. The solid shapes also suit a room that will see lots of family activity and needs to be practical and robust, as well as good-looking. There's no space for a separate shower here so an over-bath shower does the job and a curtain with a fresh, mosaic pattern protects from splashes.

Floor: Wooden boards are a great, hygienic choice for a bathroom. Here, the golden pine colour adds some warmth to this fresh scheme and ties in with the loo seat. Just make sure that boards are properly sealed and varnished to prevent splashes marking the wood or, worse still, warping it.

Accessories: There's a nice mix of pieces in this room, which gives it relaxed character without making it feel cluttered. The cistern top is home to a plant, shells, a candle and picture frame, while a vase full of elegant long twigs makes a pretty display by the window. An old Lloyd Loom chair fits in well with the room's slightly old-style feel while a modern mat adds a dash of fun to the floorboards.

The look: A simply-styled suite leaves scope for imaginative decor that makes this a colourful, family space. Vibrant blue tiles and wooden flooring laid on the diagonal bring this square room to life.

Colour: Back in the 1970s, coloured suites, from avocado to burgundy, were big style news. These days, white is the hottest colour for bathroom suites, and no wonder. It goes with any shade and looks clean, fresh and timeless. Here, it's teamed with a warm lilac on the walls (a relaxing shade, so good for lazy soaks) and vibrant blue tiles (fun and fresh – just right for kids). Pale wooden flooring adds a natural note, while all other accessories are in blue or lilac to keep the room feeling calmly coordinated.

Suite: With its smooth lines and neat shape, this suite would fit into any bathroom.

The taps have white tops for a really fresh effect and the loo cistern has a push-down flush fitted into its top, so it's extra sleek and streamlined.

Walls: Blue tiles are a winner in a bathroom, looking fresh and sea-like, just right for a room where water is key. The top row has paler tiles mixed in and dark tiles with a silver inset. This creates a pretty border and the silvery colour matches the metal of the mirror frame, shelf and towel rail. Lilac above calms the scheme down a little while keeping it colourful. A blue painting ties in perfectly with the tiles.

Flooring: Wooden flooring has been laid on the diagonal, a nifty trick that can make a square room feel less boxy and more spacious. It's a good idea in a bathroom, too, where rows of tiles create a very linear, symmetrical feel. Diagonal lines on the floor help off-set that.

STOCKISTS:

ONE-STOP SHOPS

B&Q
Major shed, catering for
every DIY need.
Tel: 0845 609 6688
www.diy.com

DEBENHAMS
Furniture, bedlinen, window
dressings and lighting.
Tel: 020 7408 4444
www.debenhams.com

FREEMANS
Furniture, bedlinen, window
dressings and lighting.
Tel: 0800 900200
www.freemans.com

HABITAT
Modern furniture, bedlinen,
lighting and storage accessories.
Tel: 0845 601 0740
www.habitat.net

HOMEBASE
All you need for DIY projects
and home decorating.
Tel: 0870 900 8098
www.homebase.co.uk

IKEA
Affordable flatpack furniture;
wall-mounted fittings; furnishings, fabrics and lighting.
Tel: 020 8208 5600
www.ikea.co.uk

JOHN LEWIS
Wide range of furniture,
fabrics, wallpapers, window
dressings, lighting and accessories. Carpet fitting service
also available.
Tel: 020 7629 7711
www.johnlewis.com

LAURA ASHLEY
Classic and country-style
furniture, fabrics, window
dressings, lighting and paints.
Tel: 0870 562 2116 for stockists,
0800 868100 for mail order
www.lauraashley.com

MARKS & SPENCER
Range of furniture, wall-
mounted fittings; towel and
bath sets; curtains, bedlinen
and lighting.
Tel: 020 7935 4422 for stockists,
0845 603 1603 for mail order
www.marksandspencer.com

NEXT HOME
Furniture, wallpaper, paints,
curtains, blinds and lighting;
bed and bath accessories.
Tel: 0870 243 5435 for stockists,
0845 600 7000 for mail order
www.next.co.uk

FLOORING

AMTICO
Quality vinyl flooring, including wood, stone and glass effects.
Tel: 0800 667766
www.amtico.com

BRINTONS
Vast range of Axminster and Wilton carpets.
Tel: 0800 505055
www.brintons.co.uk

CRUCIAL TRADING
Natural floorcoverings and rugs in sisal, coir and seagrass.
Tel: 01562 743747
www.crucial-trading.com

DALSOUPLE
Rubber flooring in many different colours.
Tel: 01278 727777
www.dalsouple.com

FIRED EARTH
Marble, slate, terracotta and ceramic floor tiles, including Roman-style mosaic effects.
Tel: 01295 814300
www.firedearth.com

FORBO-NAIRN
Practical flooring, including natural product Marmoleum.
Tel: 01592 643777
www.nairn-cushionflor.co.uk

HARVEY MARIA
PVC laminated floor tiles with funky photographic images.
Tel: 020 8516 7788
www.harveymaria.co.uk

KÄHRS FLOORING
Hardwood flooring, mostly from sustainable Swedish forests.
Tel: 01243 778747
www.kahrs.se

PERGO ORIGINAL
Range of wood-effect laminate flooring.
Tel: 0800 374771
www.pergo.com

RYALUX CARPETS
Plain and subtly patterned wool carpets that can be supplied in any width to avoid wastage.
Tel: 0800 163632
www.ryalux.carpetinfo.co.uk

TOMKINSONS CARPETS
Wide range of colours and patterns, plus jazzy borders.
Tel: 0800 374429
www.tomkinsons.co.uk

WICANDERS
High-quality wood and cork flooring in many finishes.
Tel: 01403 710001
www.wicanders.co.uk

FABRICS, PAINTS AND WALLPAPERS

ANNA FRENCH
Floral and paint-effect
wallpapers; printed cotton
fabrics, lace and sheers.
Tel: 020 7349 1099
www.annafrench.co.uk

AURO ORGANIC PAINTS
Paints and woodstains made
from natural products.
Tel: 01799 543077
www.auroorganic.co.uk

CATH KIDSTON
Retro 1950s-style floral cottons.
Tel: 020 7221 4000
www.cathkidston.co.uk

COLOROLL
Contemporary wallcoverings
and coordinating bedlinen.
Tel: 0800 056 4878
www.coloroll.co.uk

CROWN PAINTS
Vast choice, including the mix-
to-order Expressions collection.
Tel: 01254 704951
www.crownpaint.co.uk

**CROWN WALLCOVERINGS &
HOME FURNISHINGS**
Wide range of wallcoverings.
Tel: 0800 458 1554
www.ihdg.co.uk

DESIGNERS GUILD
Colourful contemporary
fabrics, wallpapers, paints
and bedlinen.
Tel: 020 7351 5775
www.designersguild.com

DULUX
Vast choice of shades in many
ranges, including the extensive
Colour Mixing System.
Tel: 01753 550555
www.dulux.co.uk

FARROW & BALL
Heritage paint shades.
Tel: 01202 876141
www.farrow-ball.co.uk

GRAHAM & BROWN
Modern wallcoverings, including
textures and metallics.
Tel: 0800 3288452
www.grahambrown.com

HAMMERITE
Paints for use on metal surfaces.
Tel: 01661 830000
www.hammerite.com

IAN MANKIN
Natural fabrics in plains, stripes
and checks; plenty of classic
tickings and ginghams.
Tel: 020 7722 0997

INTERNATIONAL PAINT
Paints and primers for tiles, melamine, radiators and floors.
Tel: 01480 484284
www.international-paints.co.uk

JANE CHURCHILL FABRICS
Wallpapers, cottons and linens with floral and geometric designs in light colours.
Tel: 020 8877 6400

KA INTERNATIONAL
Cottons in vibrant colours.
Tel: 020 7584 7352
www.ka-international.com

KNICKERBEAN
Discount stores with designer fabrics at bargain prices.
Tel: 01842 751327

MALABAR
Hand-woven silks and cotton fabrics imported from India.
Tel: 020 7501 4200
www.malabar.co.uk

THE MODERN SAREE CENTRE
Sarees and Indian silks.
Tel: 020 7247 4040

THE NATURAL FABRIC COMPANY
Wide range of natural fabrics.
Tel: 01488 684002

OSBORNE & LITTLE
Classic and contemporary prints, weaves and wallpapers.
Tel: 020 7352 1456
www.osborneandlittle.com

PLASTI-KOTE
Spray paints, including metallics, suitable for most surfaces.
Tel: 01223 836400
www.spraypaint.co.uk

SANDERSON
Extensive paint, fabric and wallpaper collections with coordinated bedlinen ranges.
Tel: 01895 830000
www.sanderson-uk.com

WILMAN INTERIORS
Contemporary and classic fabrics and wallpapers.
Tel: 01282 727300
www.wilman.co.uk

SUITES, SHOWERS AND TAPS

AQUALISA
High-performance electric, power and mixer showers.
Tel: 01959 560000
www.aqualisa.co.uk

ARMITAGE SHANKS
Suites for every setting, from cottage-style to contemporary.
Tel: 0800 866 966
www.armitage-shanks.co.uk

ASTON MATTHEWS
Wide range of baths, from roll-top to hi-tech designs, plus basins, loos and bidets.
Tel: 020 7226 7220
www.astonmatthews.co.uk

BATH DOCTOR
Restoration work carried out on antique baths and sanitaryware.
Tel: 01795 591711

BATHROOM CITY
Over 100 bathrooms on display. Good cash and carry deals.
Tel: 0121 708 0111
www.bathroomcity.co.uk

BATHROOM DISCOUNT CENTRE
Discounts on famous-name bathroom fittings.
Tel: 020 7381 4222
www.bathroomdiscount.co.uk

BATHSTORE.COM
Wide range of sanitaryware, taps and showers to buy on-line.
Tel: 07000 228478
www.bathstore.com

COLOURWASH
Contemporary designer-style fittings, including coloured glass and stainless steel basins.
Tel: 020 8947 5578
www.colourwash.co.uk

DARYL SHOWERS
Multi-spray showers; enclosures, doors and bath screens in a variety of different finishes.
Tel: 0151 606 5000
www.daryl-showers.co.uk

DOLPHIN BATHROOMS
Styles ranging from country cottage to city chic, some including furniture, with complete design and installation service.
Tel: 0800 626717
www.dolphinbathrooms.com

IDEAL-STANDARD
Wide range of contemporary and classic fittings, including suites designed to fit into small spaces.
Tel: 0800 590311
www.ideal-standard.co.uk

THE IMPERIAL BATHROOM CO
Traditional-style suites and storage furniture.
Tel: 01922 743074
www.imperial-bathrooms.co.uk

MAGNET
Modern and traditional suites, including roll-top and whirlpool baths; computer-aided planning. Branches nationwide.
www.magnet.co.uk

MATKI
Designer shower enclosures, shower trays and bath screens.
Tel: 01454 322888
www.matki.co.uk

MIRA SHOWERS
Wide range of electric, mixer and power showers.
Tel: 01242 221221
www.mira-showers.co.uk

ROYAL DOULTON
High-quality suites and taps with distinctive contemporary looks.
Tel: 01270 879777

SHIRES BATHROOMS
Wide range of classic-style suites, taps and accessories.
Tel: 01274 521199
www.shiresbathrooms.co.uk

SHOWERLUX
Wide range of shower enclosures, including some fitted with hydrotherapy jets; baths in some unusual shapes.
Tel: 024 7688 2515
www.tritonshowers.co.uk

SOTTINI
Upmarket suites in contemporary and traditional designs, including sculptural wall-hung fittings and roll-top, whirlpool and spa baths.
Tel: 0800 591586
www.sottini.co.uk

TRITON
Wide range of electric, mixer and power showers at prices to suit all pockets.
Tel: 024 7637 2222
www.triton-showers.co.uk

TWYFORD BATHROOMS
Wide range of modern, classic and Art Deco suites and taps at prices to suit every pocket.
Tel: 01270 879777
www.twyfordbathrooms.com

VITRA
Contemporary designs, with a good choice of back-to-wall and wall-hung sanitaryware.
Tel: 01235 820400

FURNITURE & STORAGE

ART IN IRON
Contemporary iron beds and matching bedside tables.
Tel: 020 7924 2332
www.zzz4u.com

THE CONRAN SHOP
Contemporary designer furniture.
Tel: 020 7589 7401
www.conran.co.uk

THE COTSWOLD COMPANY
Storage furniture and baskets in wood and woven fibres.
Tel: 01252 391404
www.cotswoldco.com

THE DORMY HOUSE
Blanket boxes and tables sold ready to paint; headboards upholstered to order.
Tel: 01264 365789
www.thedormyhouse.com

DUCAL
Solid wood furniture in traditional designs, including four posters.
Tel: 0870 742 9902
www.ducal-furniture.co.uk

FUTON COMPANY
Futon sofa beds, simple screens and canvas-covered wardrobes.
Tel: 0845 609 4455

GRAND ILLUSIONS
French country-style furniture, painted, distressed or waxed.
Tel: 020 8607 9446
www.maison.com

HAMMONDS FURNITURE
Fully fitted storage systems made to measure.
Tel: 01455 251451

THE HOLDING COMPANY
Contemporary storage furniture and accessories.
Tel: 020 8445 2888
www.theholdingcompany.co.uk

THE IRON BED COMPANY
Iron beds in classic and contemporary styles.
Tel: 01243 578888
www.ironbed.co.uk

JAY-BE
Wide range of beds, sofa beds and folding beds.
Tel: 01924 517820 for stockists, 01924 517822 for brochure
www.jaybe.co.uk

LAKELAND LIMITED
Storage fittings for organizing wardrobe and drawer space.
Tel: 01539 488100
www.lakelandlimited.co.uk

MAGNET
Fitted and freestanding furniture.
Over 500 branches nationwide –
contact local branch for details.
Tel:01325 744344
www.magnet.co.uk

MFI
Affordable furniture suites in
solid pine or wood finishes.
Tel: 0870 607 5093
www.mfi.co.uk

NORDIC STYLE
Painted wooden furniture in
classic Swedish designs.
Tel: 020 7351 1755

THE PIER
Ethnic-style furniture ranges in
dark wood, bamboo and rattan.
Tel: 0845 609 1234
www.pier.co.uk

RELYON
Traditional bedsteads in forged
iron, cast metal and brass.
Tel: 01823 667501
www.relyon.co.uk

SCUMBLE GOOSIE
Ready-to-paint furniture in
classic designs.
Tel: 01453 731305
www.scumblegoosie.com

SHAKER
Shaker-style furniture, storage
boxes and folk-art accessories.
Tel: 020 7935 9461
www.shaker.co.uk

SHARPS BEDROOMS
Fully fitted storage systems
made to measure.
Tel: 0800 917 8178

SLEEPEEZEE
Divan beds, including the back-
care collection.
Tel: 020 8540 9171

SLUMBERLAND
Divan beds, headboards,
mattresses and sofa beds.
Tel: 0161 628 2898
www.slumberland.co.uk

SOFAS AND SOFA-BEDS
Sofas and sofa beds upholstered
to order.
Tel: 020 7637 1932
www.sofaweb.co.uk

WICKES
Affordable fitted furniture
ready for DIY assembly.
Tel: 0870 608 9001
www.wickes.co.uk

LIGHTING

BHS
Stylish but affordable lights and shades in a range of styles.
Tel: 020 7384 2888
www.bhs.co.uk

CHRISTOPHER WRAY LIGHTING
Huge range of designs, from traditional to cutting edge.
Tel: 020 7736 8434
www.christopher-wray.com

JOHN CULLEN LIGHTING
Discreet modern lighting, such as spots and downlighters.
Tel: 020 7371 5400
www.johncullenlighting.co.uk

LONDON LIGHTING CO
Wide range of lighting, including downlighters, recessed spots and halogen lights.
Tel: 020 7589 3612

MCCLOUD & CO
Vast choice of light fittings by British craftspeople, available in a selection of different finishes.
Tel: 020 7352 1533
www.mccloud.co.uk

MR LIGHT
Stylish range of bathroom lighting, incuding unobtrusive halogen spotlights.
Tel: 020 7352 7525

PURVES AND PURVES
Contemporary light fittings by top European designers, plus some more affordable designs.
Tel: 020 7580 8223
www.purves.co.uk

RYNESS
Practical well-made fittings, including recessed eyeball ceiling lights, halogen spots and slimline striplights.
Tel: 01229 469600
www.ryness.co.uk

SKK LIGHTS
Innovative contemporary light fittings, including floor-mounted spotlights and minimalist-style back-lit panels.
Tel: 020 7434 4095
www.skk.net

THE STIFFKEY LAMPSHOP
Original and reproduction lamps, candlesticks and candelabra.
Tel: 01328 830460

WAX LYRICAL
Decorative candles and candleholders.
Tel: 020 8561 0235

ARTISAN
Wide range of poles and finials, from trendy to traditional.
Tel: 01772 202202

THE CURTAIN EXCHANGE
Quality secondhand curtains bought and sold.
Tel: 020 7731 8316
www.thecurtainexchange.cwc.net

LUXAFLEX
Made-to-measure blinds in modern styles, including Venetian and pinoleum.
Tel: 0161 442 9500
www.luxaflex.com

PRÊT À VIVRE
Curtains and blinds made to measure; poles and tiebacks.
Tel: 0845 130 5161
www.pretavivre.com

RUFFLETTE
Tiebacks, blind and eyelet kits and curtain-making products.
Tel: 0161 998 1811
www.rufflette.com

THE SHUTTER SHOP
Wooden shutters made to order; wooden Venetian blinds.
Tel: 01252 844575
www.shuttershop.co.uk

WINDOW TREATMENTS

ACOVA RADIATORS
Heated towel rails, towel-drying radiators and tall radiators that incorporate mirrors.
Tel: 01252 531200
www.acova.co.uk

DK HEATING SYSTEMS
Underfloor heating systems, towel warming units and fog-free backing to prevent mirrors from steaming up.
Tel: 01895 825288
www.dkheating.com

MHS RADIATORS
Traditional and modern radiator designs in various colours and finishes; heated towel rails.
Tel: 01268 591010
www.mhsradiators.co.uk

VENT-AXIA
Extractor fans and ventilation units designed for bathrooms.
Tel: 01293 526062
www.vent-axia.com

HEATING AND VENTILATION

ACCESSORIES

BEDECK
Bedlinen featuring modern florals and geometric patterns.
Tel: 0845 603 0861
www.bedeckhome.com

BLISS
Accessories with quirky shapes, such as clocks.
Tel: 01789 400077

BOMBAY DUCK
Contemporary photo frames, beaded items and more.
Tel: 020 8749 7000
www.bombayduck.co.uk

CHRISTY
Wide range of towels, plus coordinating bathmats.
Tel: 0161 368 1961
www.christy-towels.com

COLOGNE & COTTON
Pretty cotton bedlinen, luxurious towels and toiletries.
Tel: 01926 332573
www.cologneandcotton.com

COUVERTURE
Hand-embroidered and appliquéd bedlinen.
Tel: 020 7795 1200
www.couverture.co.uk

DAMASK
Pastel-coloured towels, prettily packaged perfumes and painted classic-style side tables.
Tel: 020 7731 3470
www.damask.co.uk

DESCAMPS
Quality bedlinen, including modern patterns and florals.
Tel: 020 7235 6957
www.descamps.com

DORMA
Varied range of bedlinen, from elaborately classic to plain contemporary designs, also fabric, cushions and throws.
Tel: 0161 251 4468
www.dorma.co.uk

HAF DESIGNS
Stainless steel, wall-mounted fittings, loo-brush holders and door handles in sleek contemporary designs.
Tel: 01992 505655
www.hafdesigns.co.uk

THE HAMBLEDON
Stylish accessories, including simple vases, cotton quilts and soapstone containers.
Tel: 01962 890055

MCCORD DESIGN BY MAIL
Bedlinen and cushions, storage baskets, chrome racks and rails and more.
Tel: 0870 908 7005
www.emccord.com

MONSOON HOME
Embroidered throws and cushions in colourful silks.
Tel: 020 7313 3000
www.monsoon.co.uk

OCEAN
Range of bedlinen, cushions and throws as well as storage and bathroom fittings.
Tel: 0870 242 6283
www.oceanuk.com

PEACOCK BLUE
Cotton and linen bedding including whites, ginghams and pastels.
Tel: 0870 333 1555
www.peacockblue.co.uk

SAMUEL HEATH
High-quality solid brass wall fittings and accessories, most with classic designs, available in a variety of finishes.
Tel: 0121 772 2303
www.samuel-heath.com

SHOWERAIL
Shower curtains in many sizes, some with wacky designs; transparent loo seats; accessories.
Tel: 01983 852565
www.showerail.com

TURNSTYLE DESIGNS
Ranges of wall-mounted accessories, plus decorative details such as door knobs, hooks and cord pulls.
Tel: 01271 325325
www.turnstyle-designs.com

UTOPIA
Fully fitted bathroom furniture in a range of styles and finishes, plus lighting and accessories.
Tel: 01902 406400
www.utopiagroup.com

WATER FRONT
Stylish but practical classic-style fittings made from solid brass and available in several finishes.
Tel: 0121 520 5346

THE WHITE COMPANY
Plain and embroidered bedlinen in white and cream made from top-quality linen and cotton.
Tel: 0870 160 1610
www.thewhiteco.com

DECORATIVE EFFECTS

DYLON
Fabric dyes in many colours.
Tel: 020 8663 4296
www.dylon.co.uk

THE ENGLISH STAMP COMPANY
Wall stamps and stamping tools.
Tel: 01929 439117
www.englishstamp.com

HOMECRAFTS DIRECT
Craft products by mail order.
Tel: 0116 269 7733
www.homecrafts.co.uk

HUMBROL
Makers of Glass Etch spray
(for a frosted effect on glass).
Tel: 01482 701191
www.airfix.com

JALI
Decorative MDF shelf trims and
fretwork panels; radiator covers
made to measure.
Tel: 01227 831710
www.jali.co.uk

L CORNELISSEN & SON
Aluminium, silver and gold leaf,
plus tools for gilding.
Tel: 020 7636 1045
www.cornelissen.co.uk

LIBERON
Waxes and other wood finishes.
Tel: 01797 367555

THE PAINTED FINISH
Paint effects, products and tools.
Tel: 01926 842376
www.craftychick.com

PÉBÉO
Fabric and porcelain paints.
Tel: 02380 701144
www.pebeo.com

RONSEAL
Kits for creating a woodgrain
effect; floor paints, woodstains.
Tel: 0114 246 7171
www.ronseal.co.uk

SPECIALIST CRAFTS
Wide range of craft products.
Tel: 0116 269 7711 for stockists,
0116 269 7733 for mail order
www.speccrafts.co.uk

STENCIL LIBRARY
Stencils and stencilling tools.
Tel: 01661 844844
www.stencil-library.com

THE BATHROOM SHOWROOM ASSOCIATION

Can supply details of showrooms listed among their members and free advice leaflets on shopping for a new bathroom.
Tel: 01782 747123
www.bathroom-association.org

BRITISH BLIND & SHUTTER ASSOCIATION

Information and advice on where to buy blinds and shutters.
Tel: 01827 52337
www.bbsa.org.uk

THE BRITISH DECORATORS' ASSOCIATION

Can supply a list of decorators in your area and a leaflet advising how to choose one.
Tel: 02476 353776

THE BUILDING CENTRE

Building information and advice; DIY guides available to buy; free reference library.
Tel: 020 7692 6200
www.buildingcentre.co.uk

THE LIGHTING ASSOCIATION

Advice on where to find answers to lighting queries; free buyers' guide available.
Tel: 01952 290905
www.lightingassociation.com

NATIONAL ASSOCIATION OF PLUMBING, HEATING AND MECHANICAL SERVICES CONTRACTORS

Supply lists of members and advice on plumbing and heating.
Tel: 024 7647 0626
www.licensedplumber.co.uk

NATIONAL INSPECTION COUNCIL FOR ELECTRICAL INSTALLATION CONTRACTING

Can supply lists of electricians, free leaflets and advice on lighting and electrical matters.
Tel: 020 7564 2323

NATIONAL INSTITUTE OF CARPET AND FLOOR LAYERS

Help with finding the right professionals to fit flooring.
Tel: 0115 958 3077
www.nicfltd.org.uk

THE ROYAL INSTITUTE OF BRITISH ARCHITECTS

Can send out lists of member architects in your area.
Tel: 020 7580 5533

TILE ASSOCIATION

Can supply lists of tilers and advice on how to choose and care for ceramic tiles.
Tel: 020 8663 1569
www.tiles.org.uk

ADVICE